Indigenous Experiences of Pregnancy and Birth

Funded by the Government of Canada
Financé par le gouvernement du Canada

Demeter Press
140 Holland Street West
P. O. Box 13022
Bradford, ON L3Z 2Y5
Tel: (905) 775-9089
Email: info@demeterpress.org
Website: www.demeterpress.org

Demeter Press logo based on the sculpture "Demeter" by Maria-Luise Bodirsky
<www.keramik-atelier.bodirsky.de>

Front cover photograph: Peekaboo Studio Photography

Printed and Bound in Canada

Library and Archives Canada Cataloguing in Publication

Indigenous experiences of pregnancy and birth / Hannah Tait Neufeld and Jaime Cidro, editors.

Includes bibliographical references.
ISBN 978-1-77258-135-5 (softcover)

1. Pregnancy--Canada. 2. Childbirth--Canada. 3. Motherhood--Canada. 4. Birth customs--Canada. 5. Native women--Canada--Social life and customs. 6. Pregnant women--Canada--Social life and customs. 7. Native women--Canada--Social conditions. 8. Traditional medicine--Canada. I. Tait Neufeld, Hannah, 1968-, editor II. Cidro, Jaime, editor

HQ759.I48 2017   306.874'308997071   C2017-905296-9

Indigenous Experiences of Pregnancy and Birth

EDITED BY
Hannah Tait Neufeld and Jaime Cidro

DEMETER PRESS, BRADFORD, ONTARIO

*This book is dedicated to the Indigenous women
who have shared their stories of pregnancy and birth,
along with those who are not yet able to speak of
their accounts of love and loss. Thank you for your strength
amid all you have experienced.*

Contents

Acknowledgements

This book was made possible through the contributions of many who gave their time, energy, and knowledge. We would especially like to thank Dr. Kim Anderson who has led the way for many of us and graciously provided the foreword to the book. The guidance provided by Dr. Andrea O'Reilly of Demeter Press was also instrumental in guiding us through this endeavour. We would also like to extend our gratitude toward the book's reviewers who share our enthusiasm for this topic, and the detailed work of Cheryl Nicholson, our copy editor. Finally, without the contributions of those who submitted their work to be included in this collection, we could not have achieved the depth and breadth without you. Thank you for your dedication, patience, and efforts over the duration of this project.

As mothers, we know that pregnancy, birthing, and parenting have taught us many things about ourselves and the world around us. We would especially like to acknowledge these teachings gifted to us by our own children, which guide us in our work.

Foreword

KIM ANDERSON

I WAS ALMOST THIRTY the first time I got pregnant. I had been living in Toronto for ten years, working as a researcher and educator among the large urban Indigenous community there. The pregnancy was unplanned, ending sadly and prematurely at twenty-one weeks. But it was that pregnancy, and the following two, that began a tremendous unfolding of Indigenous theories, practices, principles, protocols and teachings, which have guided me these last twenty-three years. This is because so much of who we are as Indigenous peoples can be learned through experiences of pregnancy and birth, and through how we support these experiences as communities. If we pay attention we can learn how to truly honour and sustain life, which to me is the essence of Indigeneity.

My experience with pregnancy began with awestruck and the slightly terrifying realization that I was carrying another life inside my own body; I was responsible for the growth and wellbeing of an entirely new person. Like many young Indigenous mothers, I also knew there were teachings within my culture that could help me navigate these responsibilities. And so, along with those cravings for red meat, I hungered for Indigenous knowledge. I was insecure and unsure as to where I might find it or how I might implement it. But friends, Indigenous organizations, my body, and the land offered themselves at various points to help me learn.

When I lost that first pregnancy, I went to a worker at Anishinawbe Health Toronto, an Auntie who helped me retrieve the remains from the hospital. As a Métis removed from traditional territories, I didn't have any homelands I could access or call my own. So my partner and I buried our baby on my friend's reserve, where we later returned to bury the placentas of our two children. I was thus blessed to have relationships with family and land "of the heart" in the absence of my own blood relations and territories. I was also privileged to know other women who had given birth at home with midwives because this taught me that I had choices in how I was going to deliver. My socioeconomic situation and location in the south also afforded me choice, which meant that I could birth at home in the ceremony of my own making. All of these conditions cracked open new spaces for learning, but I still felt as if I had relatively little Indigenous knowing around this sacred responsibility.

Years went by, and I continued to hunger for knowledge about women's life-giving capacities, jurisdictions, and authorities. Eventually this led to an academic research career. Now that I am entering the grandmother stage, I can reflect on what I have learned, and how this might have helped or informed me when I was in the pregnancy and birthing stage of my life. I think what has become more clear to me is the connection between women, water, and creation.

Not long after my first child was born, I began to drive out to do full moon ceremonies with my friend Valarie King at Mississaugas of New Credit First Nation. Those ceremonies, which we did together for seven years (until I started leading them for Indigenous students in Guelph), taught me so much about how women are made of cycles and seasons and how we organize and oversee kinship. Our group of women sat with rain, sleet, and snow—or fireflies and crickets— depending on which moon we were visiting. We passed through the turbulent times and celebrations of each other's lives by praying collectively for offerings, and singing and talking around the fire. I began to think about water in all its properties, the pull of grandmother moon, and the monthly cycles and ceremonies of our bodies.

In my work life, I fell into research about the connection between Indigenous women and water, and I visited Elders from different territories to help me with this question. These Elders talked about waters that are the veins of Mother Earth, and about what happens when we disrupt that flow. I learned that waters have different characteristics and purposes; like us, they go through cycles and transitions. I began to think about how water is the cradle of beginnings and that new life is always ushered in by the breaking of waters. I learned about the grandmothers that sit at the lake in the spirit world and how they send us in on a bed of water to be caught by a grandmother on this side (Anderson 2010).

One of my favourite water and life teachings comes from Maria Campbell, in a story she told about a lake in her homeland territory in Northern Saskatchewan. This lake is called Notokwew Sakahikan—the Old Lady Lake. Maria remembers that when they were children and their families visited this lake, they weren't allowed to run and splash around or enter the lake. They were to sit quietly while the old ladies lifted their long skirts and waded in to pick medicines. These were the medicines that they used in their midwifery work and in the work they did to prepare the dead for the next world. As Maria has said, "It was an old lady that brings you in, and an old lady that takes you out" (154). This story taught me so much about how women, land, water, and the honouring and sustaining of life in all its transitions are intimately connected.

As I write this, we are in the midst of water protectors by taking a stand against the Dakota Access pipeline. It seems now, more than ever, we need to honour these connections. We need to continue to educate ourselves so we can find strength and beauty in all of the work that lies ahead.

Even though I felt dispossessed of a lot of this knowledge in my younger years, I now realize that these teachings have always been there for those who go looking. Research and writing can be one way of finding them as well as a means of sharing. I would have loved books on Indigenous mothering during my pregnant and birthing years, which is why I am so happy to see this collection coming forward. In the chapters here, there are multiple entry points to critically think about the meaning of birth and pregnancy within our histories, traditions, and contemporary experiences. We might hear lots in prenatal classes about eating and exercise, but this material can help us to see how these practices become the sacred physical. We can learn here about other practices related to the life-giving body, such as seclusions during menstruation or after a birth. The authors and contributors validate practices such as burying the placenta, which we see is equally valued by Indigenous peoples on the other side of the world. We see how important it is for fathers to observe protocols and for the community to rally and support the pregnant couple. We learn how all of these things were disrupted and what we need to do to put them in place again. And we are reassured that Western medical protocols are not always the answer.

Most of all, we have many new stories here that can teach us. I am grateful to the authors and editors, for this knowledge will empower a new generation of mothers, families and communities. It is a great gift that will support us in our responsibilities and help ensure that life continues.

WORK CITED

Anderson, Kim. *Aboriginal Women, Water and Health: Reflections from Eleven First Nations, Inuit and Metis Grandmothers.* Atlantic Centre of Excellence for Women's Health and Prairie Women's Health Centre of Excellence, 2010.

Campbell, Maria. Foreword. *Life Stages and Native Women: Memory, Teachings, and Story Medicine,* by Kim Anderson, University of Manitoba Press, 2011, pp. xv-xix.

Introduction

Pregnancy and Birthing:
The Essence of Indigeneity

JAIME CIDRO AND HANNAH TAIT NEUFELD

THE BOND BETWEEN MOTHER AND CHILD is like no other relationship experienced in life. Other relationships in life other
than the mother and child relationship need to be built to become
established and continually nurtured. So do collaborations, especially if they begin in friendship. The idea for this book originated
in conversations we had about potentially working together, given
our common interests. We first met as PhD students supported
through the Aboriginal Capacity and Developmental Research
Environments (ACADRE), which later became the Network Environments for Aboriginal Health Research (NEAHR) networks
through the Canadian Institutes for Health Research (CIHR)
Institute for Aboriginal Peoples Health. At the time, Hannah was
based in Winnipeg, Manitoba, and Jaime was in Guelph, Ontario, which has subsequently become reversed in the last six years.
Through our graduate work and as new independent investigators,
our paths have overlapped. We have traversed the landscape of
maternal health, independently working with First Nation communities in both southern and northern parts of Manitoba. When
we started on this journey working on a book together, we faced
great expectations, given the range of research and scholarship
emerging in this field. It was inspiring to follow in the footsteps
of previous co-editors, Kim Anderson, D. Memee Lavell-Harvard
and Jeannette Corbiere Lavell. Their anthologies—*"Until Our
Hearts are on the Ground": Aboriginal Mothering, Oppression,
Resistance and Rebirth*, and *Mothers of the Nations: Indigenous
Mothering as Global Resistance, Reclaiming and Recovery*—laid

the groundwork for scholarship in this often ignored subject area. Kim's work with women and families over the years and her mentorship to us as friends and colleagues has also helped to shape how we understand the interplay between traditional roles of women, cultural revitalization, self-determination, as well as our own journey as mothers.

The literature and media often ignore the reassertion of Indigenous women's traditional roles; instead, they often highlight the dramatic inequalities experienced by Indigenous[1] women and their families. Researchers have documented such negative statistics as the proportion of Indigenous women and mothers who live with violence, those who do not seek prenatal care, and the number of children taken from them, but these numbers do not tell the whole story. Perpetuation of this deficit-based narrative has a detrimental effect on the path of self-determination because it fails to highlight successes. As nations such as Canada formed and became colonized, authorities saw traditional Indigenous gender roles as an impediment to successful colonization. The forced re-arrangements of these gender roles disrupted families structures, namely because they removed women from places of power. As common law became the foundation for law in colonized countries, Indigenous women quickly lost their social and legal status and became dependent on fathers and then on husbands. The traditional structures of communities became replaced with colonially informed governance, which reinforced patriarchy and paternalism. In Canada, the Indian Act, a legal instrument controlling life in First Nations communities, has reinforced the diminished roles of Indigenous women in society through the enfranchisement of Indian status through marriage and limited property rights. Other historic policies that have had devastating effects on Indigenous women include Canada's Sterilization Act. The administration of residential schools throughout Canada had an immediate effect not only on mothers but on entire families and communities, both because of the resulting social pathologies and the disruption of parenting practices. Although these schools finally shut their doors in 1996, many argue that the ongoing apprehension of children through child welfare has had an equally if not more devastating impact on women's ability to mother their own children. Although some of these programs and policies have disappeared or changed, the residue of patriarchy still remains and affects how Indigenous women are positioned and directly informs how women experience pregnancy and the birth of children. The authors in this book carefully consider these historic interactions and how they affect Indigenous women's experiences.

EXPERIENCES OF PREGNANCY

Pregnancy is a special time for women and their families. It's a time when women carefully consider their bodies as a space for the development of a life. The food a woman eats, the ceremonies and activities she participates in are no longer a focus solely for the mother, but also for the child she is carrying. These careful considerations are described in various ways by authors in this book. In chapter one, Sana Shahram, for example, argues that substance abuse among Indigenous mothers must be understood through the historic and contemporary forces shaping such behaviour. Understanding the challenges facing some pregnant Indigenous women using various substances cannot be considered without the larger context of colonization.

In the face of the challenging history of colonialism, pregnant mothers have relied on families and friends to support them in their pregnancy. In chapter two, Hannah Tait Neufeld discusses the pregnant woman's diet as having an intergenerational component. She describes women's experiences and understandings of the role of food in their pregnancy as different depending on the generation. Few scholars have explored maternal dietary beliefs, but it has become increasingly important, given the rising prevalence of lifestyle related issues such as gestational diabetes. The grandmothers Neufeld interviewed described the importance of "foods from the land" as important parts of the maternal diet. She describes the importance of prenatal nutrition grounded in a community-based approach as more effective because it is responsive to the mother's evolving Indigenous worldview.

In chapter three, Terry Rentner, Dinah Tetteh, and Lynda Dixon discuss the role of culture in the context of prenatal public health campaigns for American Indians and Native People of Alaska (AI/

AN). The cultural identity of AI/AN people is largely ignored in health campaigns, which are actually aimed at this population. Birth rates among this group are markedly high compared to the non-Hispanic (white) population in the U.S., as is the infant mortality rate. The authors describe lifestyle challenges such as obesity, smoking, and alcohol use as contributing to the high infant mortality rates. Access to prenatal care is also important for understanding the high rate of infant mortality. Rentner and colleagues describe some of the best practices of health promotion campaigns, which have been community based and have successfully integrated cultural nuances, identity, and spirituality in healthy pregnancy campaigns. Evaluation is critical to understanding the effectiveness of health promotion campaigns. Programs and campaigns must be developed with an eye on how to effectively evaluate the success of programs so that further development continues to be built on these strengths.

BIRTH, PLACE, AND LOCATION

Location of birth is often tied to homeland and, subsequently, to culture and traditions. However, for many Indigenous women living in remote and rural communities, few options exist for birthing in home communities due to relocation for birth. The literature has focused on the intersection of the impact of location for pregnancy and birth with culture and belonging across many locations both in Canada and internationally. An Indigenous woman's experiences of pregnancy and its intersection with culture and colonialism extend directly into her birth experience. Several authors describe birthing as it relates to place and culture. In chapter four, Jaime Cidro describes the experiences of women in northern Manitoba who, like many women in rural and remote communities, are evacuated prior to their due date to delivery in tertiary-care centres. The practice of maternal evacuation has come under recent scrutiny not only from communities directly but also from practitioners and policymakers who argue it has wide-reaching negative effects, specifically around maternal stress. Cidro describes some of the findings from a community-based research project, which sought to understand the possibilities for returning birthing to the community. Midwives play an important role in the movement to return birthing to communities, not only for low-risk pregnancies but also for prenatal and postnatal care. The integration of midwives into primary-care teams varies across region to region. In Norway House Cree Nation, where the research took place, Cidro discusses the same experiences of some women who left the community to give birth and the loneliness they felt. In many cases, women temporarily relocate to the city to give birth without the support of their spouse, parents and their other children. With an impending due date, women describe experiencing boredom, which also leads to stress and anxiety. The women also detail the financial implications of being forced to leave the community to give birth. Many of the women interviewed describe already experiencing financial hardship, and this is exacerbated by the added costs of relocating. Maintaining connections to their families through phone calls, buying food, and supporting family members to stay for the delivery, all place a great deal of financial stress on expectant families. Although the scope of the project is much larger than the women's experiences, the community hopes to use the information from this project to support the return of a maternity program in the community and to become self-determining in the health of their community.

First Nation women who are evacuated for birth do so as part of the obligation of the government to provide access to primary care. This practice is associated with the dominance of medical risk management through the use of biomedical knowledge and access to technologies. In chapter five, Rachel Olson describes other risks facing women moving to tertiary-care centres to birth encounter, namely the social and family risks. Her chapter is based on ethnographic fieldwork focusing on the politics of birthplace for Indigenous women in Manitoba. Olson's work took place in a large urban hospital in Winnipeg, Manitoba, where she witnessed the reality of childbirth practices for Indigenous women. She profiles three women relocated to a hospital to give birth who experience a range of risks created, realized and managed in a clinical setting. One woman had an uncomplicated birth, which did not require intervention. However, her experience highlights the social risk of not having her family or community network for support.

Another woman describes the intervention of social services into the birthing space, and the third chronicles a birth requiring an emergency Caesarean section. The hospital thereby becomes a place of medicalized regulation with complex social interactions encompassing broader notions of health, social relations, and Indigenous nationhood. These birth experience stories described by Olson help us understand that little room exists for negotiating one's birth experience within the hospital setting. For women who are evacuated, they must engage in constant negotiations of social risks. In this unfamiliar clinical setting, the biomedical risks of childbirth were given precedence over the mitigation of social risks by the health care system and policies informing care practices. The stories provide tangible examples of this complex set of negotiations between the birthing women, care providers, and policymakers.

Reclaiming a place to birth is also connected to reclaiming traditional birthing practices for Indigenous women. In chapter six, Naomi Simmonds chronicles the challenges and possibilities of reclaiming maternal knowledges and associated practices and ceremonies for Māori women and family units (*whānau*) in contemporary New Zealand. Simmonds describes how colonialism has silenced Māori women's voices and subsequent maternal knowledges, resulting in Māori women experiencing births in Western institutions under Western ideologies, which leave no room for Indigenous ways of being and birthing. Māori pregnancy and childbirth knowledges have been replaced with typically non-Māori registered midwives and mostly male doctors. Despite the predominance of midwives in New Zealand, the dominant narratives are produced in a monocultural framework that does not provide for Māori maternal knowledges. Māori women and whānau become marginalized or even invisible. Simmonds argues that the movement toward reclaiming ancient knowledges and practices is essential for transforming the individual and collective experiences of birth and afterbirth. Simmonds identifies *tikanga*—customs, traditions, practices, or ethical behaviours—as pivotal to Māori identity. Returning the placenta to the earth is one example of how tikanga is practically applied. Simmonds' participants describe their relationship to tikanga and pregnancy, birth and afterbirth. Māori families are evolving and diversifying the ways in which the whānau perform the tikanga; however, the intent of function remains. Indigenous maternal experience is an active site for process of decolonization through reclaiming the ancient messages and embodied practices of pregnancy, birth, and afterbirth.

Revitalizing traditional birthing knowledge is also considered in separate chapters by Rebeka Tabobondung, Leslie Dawson, and Margaret Macdonald. Colonialism and the powers of the Indian Agent across First Nation communities have had enormous effects on Indigenous women. The economic dominance of Indigenous men over women modelled on this patriarchal system justified surveillance by colonial authorities over such processes as reproduction and birth knowledge. Women were taught not to value this traditional knowledge as it was viewed as primitive and based on superstition. In chapter seven, Tabobondung describes the experiences of three generations of mothers on traditional birth knowledge in Wasauksing, Ontario. They share stories in which pregnancy, childbirth, and the newborn are considered sacred and honoured as central to the community. The birthing culture of the Anishnabek is complex and involves the whole community rather than just the birthing mother and father. Maintaining a good frame of mind is important because the baby can be influenced by the parent's emotions and experiences. An expectant father was highly supported by the community during his partner's pregnancy. He is restricted from hunting and fishing activities and handling dead animals so he can honour life. His family would take on these traditional roles to provide for the family. Tabobondung also describes how communities protect the expectant parents and attend to their needs, ensuring a healthy, stress-free pregnancy. The author emphasizes the importance of reclaiming and rejuvenating these forms of ancestral knowledge based on oral tradition. The persistence of these oral stories demonstrates the resilience of birth traditions for Indigenous people.

In chapter eight, Dawson writes about how changes in the birth places of the Tlicho people have been influenced by missionaries and a medicalized system. The birth experience itself becomes inscribed on Tlicho maternal bodies. She describes Tlicho's women's bodies as recipients of the processes of colonization and recommends a return to maternal practices to allow for customs of care by women during labour and childbirth to be revitalized. Traditional knowledge transfer around perinatal care could be improved when the care is provided in the woman's Indigenous mother tongue.

In chapter nine, MacDonald illustrates findings from a series of in-depth interviews with eight mothers from the Stó:lō First Nation. Her results similarly profile the importance of maternal ties to the community and the cultural traditions to childbirth, naming practices, and maternal identity. Participants' narratives, often taking the form of stories about past experiences, contribute to her construction of maternal identity and culture influenced by broader values and belief systems. MacDonald emphasizes that maternal practices considered within this cultural context illuminate that cultural transmission continues through the birth of a child. For these reasons, she suggests that the interviews with mothers with recent childbirth experiences are particularly insightful, given the contribution they make to our understanding of cultural transmission and identity formation. These narratives also constitute pathways of past and present experiences that have been woven together.

Finally, in chapter ten, Erika Finestone and Cynthia Stirbys help us reflect on the findings from the 1996 Royal Commission of Aboriginal Peoples (RCAP) and from the more recent 2015 Truth and Reconciliation Commission's (TRC) Final Report in how we understand the experiences of pregnancy and birthing from a political perspective. These reports, Finestone and Stirbys contend, clearly outline the right of Indigenous communities to access and practice their traditions. However, even though political and constitutional recognition of Indigenous customs now exists, Indigenous women's sovereignty over the birth process continues to be compromised in the Canadian context with evacuation policies, which are regularly adhered to in remote communities. They argue that acts of returning birth to communities and revitalizing Indigenous birthing practices affirm sustained resilience and strength, instead of a one-sided process of reconciliation. Therefore in deconstructing the false boundaries between politics and Indigenous women's bodies, Finestone and Stirbys suggest acknowledging the decolonized possibilities when Indigenous women are given the right to self-determination and a more equitable nation-to-nation relationship in their own unique experiences of pregnancy and birth.

CONCLUSION

The decolonized possibilities for birthing became evident in the fall of 2016 as the world watched Indigenous women from Turtle Island and beyond assert this resilience and strength. Midwives and families demonstrated the ultimate in Indigenous self-determination through the birthing of an Indigenous child at Standing Rock Reservation during the resistance to the Dakota Access Pipeline. We saw midwives and birth workers supporting women who wanted to birth in a place of tradition and ceremony, which reinforced a deep connection to land and water. Despite years of policies and practices, which have negated Indigenous maternal practices and birthing knowledge, a reclamation of the value of place and ceremony has been ignited within Indigenous women across the world, as they repossess their rights to protect water, starting with the water inside them.

This book is the result of women expressing their desires to demonstrate their inherent rights as water protectors and life givers. Decolonization acknowledges such policies as sterilization, birth evacuation and prenatal health promotion practices as being grounded in systemic racism. Emphasizing that maternal knowledge inside all of us will support Indigenous women and families toward fulfilling self-determination during this sacred time and moment in history.

ENDNOTE

[1]The term "Indigenous" is used throughout this book to describe the Indigenous Peoples of Canada, the United States, and New Zealand and their descendants. In Canada, Aboriginal, First Nation, Inuit and Métis are all recognized in the Constitution Act of Canada, whereas in the U.S. American Indian and Alaska Native are used. The Māori are the original peoples of Aotearoa.

I. Pregnancy

1.
Indigenous Pregnancy, Birthing, and Mothering in Colonial Canada

SANA Z. SHAHRAM

INDIGENOUS MOTHERS IN CANADA have endured much scrutiny by researchers, health professionals, and the general public on the issue of alcohol and drug use during pregnancy (Shahram 158). However, although researchers and policy makers have focused much attention on the identification and quantification of substance use[1] among Indigenous women in Canada, much less attention has been paid to understanding the complex intersections between colonial processes and Indigenous women's experiences with pregnancy and mothering. This chapter presents a detailed overview of the history of Indigenous mothering in Canada, with a focus on colonization practices that have dramatically altered their traditional social locations. Researchers need to examine issues such as racism, addiction, poverty, precarious social and medical status, violence, chronic social and legal persecution, and discrimination from an understanding of the effects of historic and contemporary colonization practices and policies (Cull 150). Failure to acknowledge the effects of specific drivers of health inequalities for young Indigenous women in Canada allows paternalistic and prejudiced attitudes toward Indigenous women to persist (Chansonneuve and Indigenous Healing Foundation 5), and serves to support mainstream society's continued ignorance of the issues and challenges facing many Indigenous women in Canada today.

Indigenous women in Canada are a diverse and varied population. However, in Canada, the term "Indigenous" is usually understood to represent peoples with First Nations, Inuit, or Métis ancestry as a ubiquitous group not requiring distinction. Although

13

great variation exists even *within* these different classifications, on account of historic and contemporary colonization practices, as well as imposed *mis*classifications, many Indigenous women share common experiences of the loss of land, language and sociocultural resources; therefore, they face a similar experience of systemic racism, discrimination, and social exclusion in the Canadian context (Halseth 1). Many Indigenous women experience similar poor health outcomes because of these social and historical circumstances, despite cultural and individual variations. As such, the determinants of substance use in relation to Indigenous women in Canada's experiences of pregnancy, birthing, and mothering, are often also similar, and this precedes the decision to consider Indigenous women as a collective population for the purposes of this chapter.

The Historical, Political, and Social Contexts of Substance Use

Explicitly acknowledging the legacy of colonial processes is a necessary starting point for understanding the root causes of substance use during pregnancy and for the development and implementation of programs and policies to serve Indigenous women (Hackett S19). As such, the contemporary socioeconomic conditions that characterize the lives of many Indigenous women in Canada today must be framed as the downstream effects of policies and processes that began with colonization (Cull 153; Halseth 2; Reading and Wien 8). Colonization practices have altered and subsumed Indigenous women's traditional social location, which has had enduring effects on their contemporary social status and health outcomes that continue to resonate in their lives today.

1.1 PRE-CONTACT INDIGENOUS WOMEN

Pre-contact Indigenous women in North America enjoyed considerable power, social status, respect, and influence (Barman 92). They were treated with reverence, as the givers of life. They were seen as the keepers of tradition, practices, and customs, and the decision makers in realms of family, property rights, and education (Boyer 69; Chansonneuve and Indigenous Healing Foundation 15). The majority of Indigenous cultures were matrilineal, and clans consisted of a Clan Mother, with her daughters or a group of sisters, together with their husbands and children (Boyer 70; Chansonneuve and Indigenous Healing Foundation 19). Rather than matrimony or divorce, mutual consent decided unions and dissolutions, while the values of noninterference and sharing guided most interactions (Chansonneuve and Indigenous Healing Foundation 19). Contrary to popular misrepresentations, precolonial Indigenous cultures in Canada had elaborated political systems, whose influences can still be seen in political organizations today. Politically, Indigenous women enjoyed sweeping powers: they ran local clan councils, ran funerals, nominated and impeached all political representatives, appointed warriors, declared war, negotiated peace, and mediated disputes (Boyer 71).

The more egalitarian structures of most Indigenous groups prior to colonization meant that women were not solely dependent on their spouses for essential needs and, were, therefore not vulnerable to violence, abuse, and domination (Cull 143). Men left their families to join their new wives' families. Women, meanwhile, controlled the economy through the distribution of wealth and inheritance, and acted as the heart and the head of their family units (Cull 143). Colonialism's progression, however, greatly diminished the status of Indigenous women (Boyer 72).

1.2 THE COLONIAL LEGACY

Beginning in the sixteenth century, European missionaries and settlers arrived in North America. Europeans subscribed to the "doctrine of discovery," which stated that sovereignty could be immediately claimed over barren or uninhabited land. If people inhabited the land, however, seizing the land required proof that those people were uncivilized and incapable of legitimately holding land (Boyer 73; Wesley-Esquimaux 19). The overall goal of colonization was land acquisition; thus, Indigenous women (who were the chief proprietors of land) became a threat to colonization (Cull 142; Boyer 73). Accordingly, Indigenous peoples' established and complex government and social systems were tactically dismantled, and male-female social roles were disrupted through the imposition of patriarchal ideals and male dominance in a concerted effort to destabilize the role of Indigenous women in Canada (Boyer 70; Cull 142; Wesley-Esquimaux 18).

The forced rearrangement of gender roles through colonization disrupted Indigenous family structures and removed women from powerful positions (Wesley-Esquimaux 18). A substantial cultural shift occurred when European fur traders refused to trade with Indigenous women. Their husbands, brothers, and fathers took over this duty; men became in charge of these trades, and women became dependent on men for their economic security (Boyer 73). The effects of the subsequent degradation of Indigenous women's social roles through colonization and postcolonial practices can be seen today in their severely compromised health status in Canada (Bourassa, McKay-McNabb, and Hampton 24). Although colonization was destructive for all Indigenous peoples in Canada, the specific damages it inflicted upon Indigenous women remains rarely discussed (Wesley-Esquimaux 20). Many of these harms have been committed through discriminatory legislation, laws, and policies.

Legislative Genocide

Colonial laws and policies disproportionately targeted and disenfranchised Indigenous women (Boyer 72). Through colonialism, male-centred values were imposed and used to shape institutions, laws, policies, and legislated discriminations, which have had continued and long-lasting negative effects on the health of Indigenous women (Boyer 73; Greenwood et al. 7). With the imposition of British common law, Indigenous women were viewed as chattels, with no social or legal status, dependent first on their fathers and then on their husbands. Married women essentially occupied the same social status as "idiots" and children (Boyer 72). Needless to say, as patriarchy and paternalism became dominant features of Indigenous societies, women's roles within Indigenous family units were annihilated (Boyer 75), as was their sense of cultural identity.

The imposition of definitions of "Indian" identity by colonialists created cultural ambiguity for Indigenous peoples. And because of the sexist specifications inherent in the legislation, the legislation's ramifications affected Indigenous women the most (Bourassa et al. 24). Some of the most severe effects on Indigenous women can be seen by examining legislation such as the Indian Act, the

Sexual Sterilization Act, and the progression of laws surrounding prostitution.

2.1 THE INDIAN ACT

Colonial legislation dramatically changed the lives of Indigenous women. In 1850, when the first legislation governing Indigenous peoples' lives in Canada was created, the term "Indian" was legally defined. This definition was formally entrenched through The Indian Act of 1876, which deemed Indigenous people to be wards of the state, entrenched a system of dependency that continues to persist today. It helped solidify predominant conceptualizations of Indigenous people as inherently inferior and incapable of independent thought (Bourassa et al. 24). Although these stereotypes began as a result of the European desire to accumulate land, Canadians, by and large, have accepted the Act's classifications as cultural in nature. The reality that these social constructions have their origins in colonial legislation has been completely forgotten (Bourassa et. 24).

Section three of the Indian Act exclusively defines an Indian as any male person of Indian blood, any child of such person, and any woman who is or was lawfully married to such a person. In 1906, an amendment to the Indian Act further redefined a person as anyone other than an Indian (Boyer 74). By defining Indigenous women as legal nonpersons until 1951 and making their Indian status dependent on their matrimonial status, the Indian Act completely destabilized the Indigenous woman's place in society (Bourassa et al. 25; Boyer 74; Cull 143).

The Indian Act reinforced racist and sexist policies in many ways, and as a consequence, diminished the power and resources available to Indigenous women in Canada (Bourassa, McKay-McNabb, and Hampton 25; Boyer 75; Cull, 2006). Until 1985 (when the Act was amended through Bill C-31 after Indigenous women lobbied to the Supreme Court and to international courts), Indian women who married non-Indian men lost their Indian status and band membership (Bourassa et al. 26; Boyer 85; Chansonneuve and Indigenous Healing Foundation 9; Cull 144; Lavell and Lavell-Harvard 8). Women were banished from their lands and communities

(as non-Indians were not allowed on reserves) and were forced
into enfranchisement (Bourassa et al. 26; Boyer 78). Even then,
"Indian" women did not receive the full benefits of Canadian
citizenship. They could not own property, and since they could
not return to the reserve even in cases of divorce, they effectively
lost all property rights (Bourassa et al. 27). Indian women who
married non-Indian men could not even inherit their husband's
land or assets after his death until 1884, after which they could
only inherit one third of the property if they were deemed to be
of "good moral character" by an Indian Agent (Bourassa et al.
25). On the flip side, if a non-Indian woman married an Indian
man, she gained full status, and retained it even after divorce or
becoming a widow (Bourassa et al. 25).

Through the gender discrimination inherent in the Indian Act, the
government committed an act of cultural genocide in which over
twenty-five thousand women lost their status and were forced to
leave their communities between 1876 and 1985 (Bourassa et al. 25;
Boyer 84; Cull 141). Even after Bill C-31 and the reinstatement of
many women to legal status, damage from the previous legislation
persisted; "new Indians," "paper Indians," or "C-31s" remained
blocked from full participation in their communities and could not
take part in the government and decision-making processes that
nonetheless affected their day-to-day lives (Bourassa et al. 27). Still
today, under Bill C-31, grandchildren and great-grandchildren of
women who marry non-status men lose their status (Bourassa,
McKay-McNabb, and Hampton 27), whereas the same does not
apply to men. The Indian Act, however, is unfortunately just one
example of discriminatory legislation perpetuated against Indigenous women in the years following colonization.

2.2 PROSTITUTION

In 1839, when the first statute that dealt with prostitution was
passed in Lower Canada, "the Native woman prostitute" was
identified as the new social problem. What had once been considered acceptable sexual relations between colonial elites and
Indigenous women during the fur trade era was replaced and
censured with prostitution (Boyer 77). Starting in 1879, several

provisions regarding prostitution were added to the Indian Act and were aimed exclusively at intra-racial prostitution only, and criminalized Indian women for practising prostitution and Indian men for pimping or purchasing the services of these women (Boyer 77). Conversely, little effort was made to punish non-Indigenous man (Boyer 78). By 1892, when the Criminal Code was developed, legislators moved prostitution from the Indian Act to the Criminal Code, and women arrested for these crimes were banished from cities and towns back to their reserves, if their communities would accept them (Boyer 78). Thus, the misrepresentation of the Indigenous woman as prostitute and as the source of "immorality" became entrenched into Canadian society. The resulting vulnerability of Indigenous women on account of these legislative practices has been exploited by Indigenous and non-Indigenous men to carry out acts of extreme brutality against Indigenous women that continue today (Boyer 79). Sexist stereotypes and racist attitudes toward Indigenous women and girls have compounded these desperate circumstances; the general indifference to their welfare and safety is blatantly evident in Canada's inadequate response to over one thousand Indigenous women who have been murdered or gone missing over the last twenty years (Boyer 82). The Sterilization Act is yet another example of Canada's attempt to control the bodies of Indigenous women through legislation.

2.3 STERILIZATION

Around 1929, with the eugenics movement gaining popularity in Europe, Canada began a policy of involuntary surgical sterilization, which was practised between 1929 and 1972 (Boyer 76). The act intended to stop "mentally defective" peoples from having children, although a 1937 amendment also applied the law to people who were deemed "incapable of intelligent parenthood" (a concept that had at this point been applied to all Indigenous mothers through the imposition of residential schools) (Boyer 76). Indigenous women were the most overrepresented group of people sterilized during this period (Boyer 76). An investigation in the United States found that between 1973 and 1976, 3,406 involuntary sterilizations of Indigenous women had occurred in just four hospitals, which at the time, given the small Indigenous population, would have been the equivalent of 500,000 women among the general population (Boyer 76). With the eugenics movement, Indigenous women's position as a population group with severely compromised status was cemented, and the precedent for placing Indigenous women's capacity to reproduce under government scrutiny was set (Cull 148).

Mothering Under the State's Gaze

The historic and contemporary practices of forcibly removing Indigenous children from their families have caused difficulties in forming trusting relationships from generation to generation (Chansonneuve, "Addictive Behaviours" 20). This difficulty in forming strong attachments as children and the experiences of historical and contemporary trauma characterizing the lives of many Indigenous women and children have contributed to addictive behaviours in Indigenous populations today (Chansonneuve, "Addictive Behaviours" 21).

Since colonization, Indigenous mothers have been unjustly characterized as unfit or inferior parents by the state, as a means to justify the continued scrutiny the government employs in its surveillance and intervention into Indigenous mothering (Cull 146). Because of its long history, the stereotype of the unfit Indigenous mother has become embedded in Canadian social and governmental systems, and this has had devastating effects for Indigenous mothers, their children, and their communities (Cull 147).

The state's interference in Indigenous pregnancies and births, beginning with colonization, stole the autonomy of Indigenous women. Instead, Indigenous women continue to navigate their experiences of motherhood under the constant and unrelenting gaze of the state (Cull 141; Simpson 25). These surveillance and intervention practices have created an enduring identity for Indigenous mothers, one often described as bad, uncivilized, or incapable. These characterizations underscore the aggressive tactics used to restrict and redefine Indigenous women's capacities in Canada (Cull 143), first through residential schools and then through child apprehension.

3.1 RESIDENTIAL SCHOOLING

Between the late 1800s and 1998, Indigenous children were forcibly removed from their homes to attend residential schools. The Canadian state created these residential schools an effort to "civilize the Indian," and since the state believed adults were already too far gone to be rescued, the schools targeted "Indian" children in the hopes of saving them from their otherwise, as they saw it, destitute fate (Chansonneuve, "Addictive Behaviours" 10; Fournier and Crey 54; Milloy 26). The residential school system was explicitly devised as a method to "kill the Indian in the child," which required the children be isolated from their so-called immoral surroundings, including their families, their communities, and their culture (Milloy 27). Residential schooling intended to indoctrinate the children into the ways of Canadian society; however, to be clear, the residential schooling curriculum never aspired beyond preparing these children to join the lowest fringes of society (Chansonneuve, "Addictive Behaviours" 11; Fournier and Crey, 51).

In what followed as one of Canada's most reprehensible crimes, children in residential schools were exposed to continued and repeated physical, sexual, and emotional abuses. They were subject to disparaging neglect on the part of the government and churches, often for the entirety of their childhoods and formative years, and sometimes for up to five generations in just one family (Fournier and Crey 7). Today, many social and health issues experienced by Indigenous peoples in Canada can be, at least in part, attributed to this long, unbroken history of abuse, mistreatment, and neglect (Chansonneuve, "Addictive Behaviours" 13; Fournier and Crey 49; Milloy 295). The sexual abuses committed against children in residential schools spilled back into their communities, and echoed in the lives of subsequent generations of children (Milloy 296). Residential schools left in their wake communities overflowing with people suffering from unhealed trauma, grief and rage, resulting in high rates of addictive behaviours, suicide, violence, and lateral violence persisting across generations (Chansonneuve, "Addictive Behavours" 12).

Residential schooling disrupted the transference of parenting skills from one generation to the next (Milloy 299). These children learned that power was exerted through abuse; moreover, they did not form stable attachments, and were shamed into hating their own identities (Chansonneuve, "Addictive Behaviours" 19; Milloy 295). These children often grew up to use these same tools on their own children and, thus, created an intergenerational cycle of harm, which persists today.

The bond between Indigenous mothers and children has been under attack for over five generations: first through the removal of children to attend residential schools and then through the apprehension of children through the child welfare system. The removal of children between 1876 and 1996 was so extreme that it is widely considered an act of cultural genocide, and these removals have served to support and sustain the notion of the "unfit" Indigenous mother in Canadian society (Cull 141). Any suggestion, however, that these practices are relics of the past is completely misplaced. Currently, Indigenous children are still overrepresented in state care; in 2011, Indigenous people represented 4.3 percent of Canada's total population, yet almost half (48.1 percent) of the thirty thousand children in foster care in Canada were Indigenous (Statistics Canada).

3.2 CHILD APPREHENSIONS

In 1951, amendments to the Indian Act transferred the responsibility of Indigenous health and welfare services to provincial jurisdiction (Cull 144). One by-product of this change was that Ottawa transferred money to the provinces based on each Indigenous child that was apprehended, resulting in what is now referred to as the "Sixties Scoop" (Cull 145). In 1955, less than 1 percent of Indigenous children resided in state care, but by 1969, the number had jumped to 40 percent. Such an increase in numbers created a "lost generation," as children were removed en masse and taken to distant communities and often never heard from again (Cull 145). Prior to the amendment, and subsequent funding, provinces cared little about Indigenous children's welfare. Moreover, American adoption agencies bought Indigenous children from Canadian child welfare services, reportedly paying between five and ten thousand dollars per child (Cull 146). Even today, 40 percent of all Indigenous children remain in state care. The justification for these child apprehensions and the surveillance of Indigenous mothers continues to be highly problematic.

Canadian child welfare agencies have been characterized by a lack of transparency, partly because of departmental policies and fragmented services that prevent systematic and critical assessments and evaluations of their activities (Cull 146). Despite these issues, it is clear that Indigenous children and youth are overrepresented at every stage of child welfare investigations (Cull 146). This overrepresentation could stem from the fact that many of the policies operate from a Western ideal of parenting, and the more an Indigenous mother deviates from this norm, the more vulnerable she becomes to state observation (Cull 147). Modern Canadian society has linked parental ability and capacity to material goods and conditions, with variables such as size of home and number of bathrooms factoring into the determination of parental negligence (Cull 147). As Cull astutely points out, the system ensures that Indigenous mothers will be deemed as negligent or incompetent. The compromised socioeconomic status of Indigenous mothers places them in perpetual risk of state intervention:

> They live their lives in a society that essentially makes poverty a "quasi" crime and Indigenous ethnicity a risk factor. Indigenous mothers, especially impoverished, multiparous, young women, must prove that they are "fit" parents on a daily basis. In criminal law terms, they are guilty and must continually prove themselves innocent. (Cull 147)

Contrary to the beliefs of child welfare agencies, research has consistently suggested that child neglect is actually a resource-based, poverty-related problem rather than a mother's choice to purposefully neglect her children (Lavell and Lavell-Harvard 185). Despite these findings, the scrutiny placed on Indigenous women continues to perpetuate situations in which women and families are set up for failure. The state's unforgiving and often merciless gaze often forces Indigenous women to conceal their problems. Instead of seeking help, they fear further intervention from the state, including having their children removed (Cull 150; Lavell and Lavell-Harvard 192; Simpson 28).

These fears are especially justified considering the 1997 court case involving an Indigenous woman who was using substances during pregnancy. In the case of *Winnipeg Child and Family Services (W.C.F.S.) v. G (D.F.) 1997*, the Winnipeg child welfare agency petitioned the detainment of an Indigenous mother, who was sniffing glue, in substance treatment until the end of her pregnancy to protect her fetus (Cull 149). The media covering the case demonized the mother as a selfish villain, and completely ignored her history—which included the woman's several attempts to receive treatment and her subsequent denial on account of limited resources as well as her limited supports as a poor, single mother (Cull 150). This case further reinforced the fact that Indigenous women seemingly have two choices when it comes to substance use during pregnancy: concealment or exposure to extreme state intervention, and the subsequent scorn of society.

In summary, the removal of children from Indigenous families for over two centuries has created a vicious cycle, which has resulted in numerous social pathologies for both parents and children. Problems such as substance use, high suicide rates and poverty have been attributed to residential schools (Shahram 159). These problems have been further exacerbated by the increased surveillance of Indigenous mothers and their children, resulting in an increased involvement with the criminal justice system and child protection agencies (Cull 151). This legacy of the removal of children from Indigenous families has contributed to and compounded the experiences of historical and intergenerational trauma characterizing the lives of many young Indigenous women who use drugs and alcohol during pregnancy. It also highlights the incredible resilience that Indigenous women and mothers have shown in response to the unthinkable acts committed by the state.

Historic and Intergenerational Trauma

Indigenous women suffer from disproportionately higher levels of sexual and physical abuse and violence in their lives (Haskell and Randall 91). In addition, researchers have stressed historical and intergenerational trauma as explanatory factors for the large health inequalities persisting among Indigenous peoples in Canada, resulting from a history of systemic racism, policies of assimilation and cultural genocide (Mitchell and Maracle 14). Scholars have described aspects of the lives of Indigenous peoples in Canada as being marked by ongoing traumatic events related such things as assimilatory policies leading to the loss of land, the decades of incarceration of Indigenous children, and the high levels of child sexual abuse, sexual assault, and domestic violence in many Indigenous communities (Haskell and Randall 50).

Indigenous mothers and their children often represent the literal site of intergenerational trauma. Recurrent recollections of trauma experienced by individuals have entered into social narratives of Indigenous peoples and have manifested in the breakdown of families and relationships, leaving children often psychologically damaged (Wesley-Esquimaux 19). Many adult survivors coping with horrifying memories have difficulty with social and parental obligations, and many women, unable to speak of their traumas, often find themselves equally unable to express love or tenderness (Wesley-Esquimaux 20; Chansonneuve, "Addictive Behaviours" 22). This sense of loneliness and trauma has, in some instances, been passed down to Indigenous women's children while they continue to try and cope with their own losses. As Wesley-Esquimaux explains: "In some instances, their bodies have become things over which they have little control, due to their own lifetime experiences of sexual and physical abuse. In their numbness, some have abused their own bodies by drinking themselves into oblivion or sniffing glue or gasoline" (21).

In these contexts, alcohol and drug use appear to be symptoms, with abuse, trauma, and social conditions as underlying causes of the behaviours (Benoit et al. 831; Chansonneuve, "Addictive Behaviours" 13). Many of these issues, again, originate in the colonial practices exerted on Indigenous families, particularly through residential schools. As Deborah Chansonneuve explains, "The toxic mixture of physical and sexual abuse, combined with racist cultural denigration and religious fundamentalism or fanaticism, proved highly traumatic for Indigenous children who attended these schools, as well as for their descendants" ("Addictive Behaviours" 41).

Contemporary health and social problems for Indigenous women and peoples in general are directly linked to the abuse suffered in residential schools—the children who were disconnected from families and communities and who were taught to feel shame about their language, customs, and heritage (Chansonneuve, "Addictive Behaviours" 42). One painful outcome of this history is lateral violence, in which oppressed groups who feel helpless against their oppressor channel anger toward one another through shaming, humiliating, and sometimes violent behaviour (Chansonneuve, "Addictive Behaviours" 12).

Considering the deep-rooted and pervasive effects that trauma has played in the lives of many Indigenous women, one cannot research substance use among Indigenous mothers without a firm understanding of its role. Due diligence must be taken not only to acknowledge the role of trauma in addictive behaviours but also to create safe spaces limiting the risks of retraumatizing participants. One major barrier to addictions services for Indigenous women is the overly specialized and fragmented nature of the services themselves, which risk retraumatizing women by requiring them to participate in numerous disclosures at multiple intakes (Chansonneuve and Indigenous Healing Foundation 6). As such, trauma-informed approaches to conducting research with Indigenous women are essential.

In understanding Indigenous women's experiences, researchers need to acknowledge the concept of resilience as the ways individuals and communities overcome these enduring hardships and traumas (Kirmayer et al. 399). Exploring resilience involves considering the "unique dimensions of development and adaptation that may contribute to human flourishing (Kirmayer et al. 399). Although traditional psychological approaches to understanding resilience have focused on individual personality traits or characteristics, researchers have also conceptualized resilience to have systemic, collective, and communal dimensions (Kirmayer et al. 400). When looking at resilience in Indigenous populations, researchers should note the dynamic systems that may confer resilience on individuals and communities in a more holistic way (Kirmayer et al. 401).

Each of the specific determinants of health for Indigenous women points to potential sources or strategies for resilience (Kirmayer et al. 401), which may include continued use of alcohol and drugs. Instead of focusing exclusively on vulnerability and pathology, a focus on resilience shifts the attention to the resources, strengths, and positive outcomes in women's lives (Kirmayer et al. 401) while highlighting opportunities to foster and support resilience through policies and interventions.

MOVING FORWARD

The evidence in Canada overwhelmingly rejects the notion that simply being Indigenous is a risk factor for poor health; still, the current funding of programmes and policies in Canada continues to reinforce this concept by prioritizing interventions continually targeted at Indigenous peoples to help *them* be healthier. Instead, the evidence consistently points to imposed legislative and social conditions that have resulted in the marginalization of Indigenous peoples. Intervening at the level of these conditions provides a promising direction for promoting health equity among Indigenous women in Canada, particularly as it relates to experiences of pregnancy, birthing and mothering and for women who use substances.

A CIHR Doctoral Research Award (CIHR Funding Number: 121268) supported the initial research and development of this content. Postdoctoral research funding through the Equity Lens in Public Health Research Project (CIHR Funding Number: 116688) supported the development of this manuscript for submission.

ENDNOTE

[1]Substance use refers to the consumption of alcohol and/or illicit drugs.

WORKS CITED

Barman, Jean. "Indigenous Women and Feminism on the Cusp of Contact." *Indigenous Women and Feminism: Politics, Activism, Culture,* edited by Cheryl Suzack et al., University of British Columbia Press, 2010, pp. 92-108.

Benoit, Cecilia, et al. "In Search of a Healing Place: Indigenous Women in Vancouver's Downtown Eastside." *Social Science & Medicine*, vol. 56, no. 4, 2003, pp. 821-33.

Bourassa, Carrie, et al. "Racism, Sexism and Colonialism: The Impact on the Health of Indigenous Women in Canada." *Canadian Woman Studies*, vol. 24, no. 1, 2004, pp. 23-30.

Boyer, Yvonne. "First Nations Women's Contributions to Culture and Community through Canadian Law." *Restoring the Balance: First Nations Women, Community, and Culture*, edited by Gail Guthrie Valaskakis et al., University of Manitoba Press, 2009, pp. 69-96.

Chansonneuve, Deborah. *Addictive Behaviours among Indigenous People in Canada*. Indigenous Healing Foundation, 2007.

Chansonneuve, D. and Indigenous Healing Foundation. *Reclaiming Connections: Understanding Residential School Trauma among Indigenous People: A Resource Manual*. Indigenous Healing Foundation, 2005.

Cull, Randi. "Indigenous Mothering under the State's Gaze." *"Until Our Hearts Are on the Ground": Indigenous Mothering, Oppression, Resistance and Rebirth*, edited by Dawn Memee Lavell-Harvard and Jeanette Corbiere Lavall, Demeter Press, 2006, pp. 141-56.

Fournier, Suzanne, and Ernie Crey. *Stolen from Our Embrace: The Abduction of First Nations Children and the Restoration of Indigenous Communities*. Douglas & McIntyre Ltd, 1997.

Greenwood, Margo, et al. "Indigenous Children and Early Childhood Development and Education in Canada: Linking the Past and the Present to the Future." *Canadian Journal of Native Education*, vol. 30, no. 1, 2007, pp. 5-18.

Hackett, Paul. "From Past to Present: Understanding First Nations Health Patterns in a Historical Context." *Canadian Journal of Public Health/Revue Canadienne de Sante'e Publique*, vol. 96, no. 1, January-February 2005, pp. S17-S21.

Halseth, Regine. *Indigenous Women in Canada, Gender, Socio-Economic Determinants of Health, and Initiatives to Close the Wellness-Gap*. National Collaborating Centre for Indigenous Health, 2013.

Haskell, Lori, and Melanie Randall. "Disrupted Attachments: A

Social Context Complex Trauma Framework and the Lives of Indigenous Peoples in Canada." *Journal of Indigenous Health*, vol. 5, no. 3, 2009, pp. 48-99.

Kirmayer, Laurence J., et al. "Toward an Ecology of Stories: Indigenous Perspectives on Resilience." *The Social Ecology of Resilience: A Handbook of Theory and Practice*, edited by Michael Ungar, Springer, 2012, pp. 399-414.

Lavell-Harvard, Dawn Memee, and Jeannette Corbiere Lavall, editors. "Introduction." *Until Our Hearts Are on the Ground": Indigenous Mothering, Oppression, Resistance and Rebirth*, Demeter Press, 2006, pp.1-13.

Milloy, John S. *A National Crime: The Canadian Government and the Residential School System, 1879 to 1986*. University of Manitoba Press, 1999.

Mitchell, Terry L., and Dawn T. Maracle. "Post-Traumatic Stress and the Health Status of Indigenous Populations in Canada." *International Journal of Indigenous Health*, vol. 2, no. 1, 2005, pp. 14-23.

Reading, Charlotte Loppie, and Fred Wien. *Health Inequalities and the Social Determinants of Indigenous Peoples' Health*. National Collaborating Centre for Indigenous Health, 2009.

Shahram, Sana. "The Social Determinants of Substance Use for Indigenous Women: A Systematic Review." *Women & Health*, vol. 56, no. 2, 2016, pp. 157-76.

Simpson, Leanne. "Birthing an Indigenous Resurgence: Decolonizing our Pregnancy and Birthing Ceremonies." *"Until Our Hearts Are on the Ground": Indigenous Mothering, Oppression, Resistance and Rebirth*, edited by Dawn Memee Lavell-Harvard and Jeanette Corbiere Lavall, Demeter Press, 2006, pp. 25-33.

Wesley-Esquimaux, Cynthia C. "Trauma to Resilience: Notes on Decolonization." *Restoring the Balance: First Nations Women, Community, and Culture*, edited by Gail Guthrie Valaskakis et al., University of Manitoba Press, 2009, pp. 13-34.

2.
"It's in Her Health"

Historical Retrospective of Generational Changes in Maternal Diets from Peguis, First Nations

HANNAH TAIT NEUFELD

THIS RESEARCH PROJECT undertaken in 2001 focused on traditional food patterns and prenatal dietary beliefs in Peguis First Nation. A series of qualitative interviews were conducted with young mothers as well as grandmothers in this southern Manitoba community to examine maternal dietary traditions, as well as food usage, local availability, and how these factors have changed across the generations. In addition, three nutritious food baskets were priced locally to compare with food costs in the closest urban centre, Winnipeg. Both types of data were used to explore cultural idea systems related to the following: maternal diet; the importance of traditional food consumption during pregnancy; changes in access to traditional foods; local food security; and the extent to which diabetes is a concern to women in the community (Neufeld, *Prenatal Dietary Reflections* 2). This chapter describes generational differences in dietary advice during pregnancy that existed when this study was originally conducted over fifteen years ago.

BACKGROUND

The way in which people conceptualize food and its relationship to health and illness can reflect dominant societal values, particularly during times of transition, such as pregnancy (Murcott 73). Prior to conducting this research, very few studies existed describing changes in maternal dietary beliefs of North American Indigenous women. Although the Nutrition Canada Survey carried out between 1970 and 1972 provides some evidence of nutrient concerns during pregnancy among Indigenous women in Canada, a low response rate made the findings less than conclusive (Canada 8; Moffatt 378). Food restrictions and specific prescriptions related to the overall wellbeing of the fetus were noted during the same period in a study that examined past and present childcare patterns among Indigenous women in the Great Lakes region of the United States (Hildebrand 35). A Canadian author described childbearing practices of the Salish First Nation in coastal British Columbia and gave examples of traditional teachings during pregnancy that included reference to similar restrictions of certain foods (Clarke 24). More recent publications on Indigenous maternal diets have tended to focus on nutrient adequacy and the prevention of prenatal weight gain (O'Driscoll et al. 26) and chronic conditions such as gestational diabetes (GDM) (Giroux et al. 128; Neufeld, "Food Perceptions" 483; Schaefer et al. 455; Vallianatos et al. 104). Still, little research has been published in the area of North American Indigenous maternal dietary behaviours. As a result, a cross-cultural review of select relevant publications will be presented to provide a historical perspective.

MATERNAL DIETARY BEHAVIOURS

Food is always defined culturally; powerful cultural elements often shape food selection throughout the life cycle. Various prescriptions and proscriptions, for example, may be directly related to the circumstances of individuals with regard to what they are, or are not, to eat (Murcott 68-9). Altered bodily states, such as pregnancy, are associated with unique dietary patterns. Changes in appetite and perceptions of food are intimately connected with the bodily experiences of pregnancy. Various cultural groups also exhibit practices and customs related to their unique belief systems surrounding nutrition and health. The sum of these attitudes, beliefs, customs, and taboos affecting the diet of a given group is defined as "food ideology" (Fieldhouse 43). These ideologies describe how foods are perceived, including how a particular food may affect health or may be suitable for certain demographic groups or life stages. A complex set of cohesively held group attitudes and values influence food belief systems. These systems may also be closely associated with ideas of illness, age, and physiological states, such as pregnancy (Sanjur 164).

In addition to being influenced by physiological needs as well as social needs and forces, food consumption during pregnancy can also be connected to emotional needs and sensations. Patterns of eating behaviours can adapt to relieve anxiety or tension in addition to providing security and comfort (Fieldhouse 206-7, 209). Foods can acquire particular associations, which greatly determine their categorization as pleasant or unpleasant. These judgments or perceptions regarding food acceptability or nonacceptability are often pronounced and can take on unique associations.

One study describes, for example, that if a pregnant woman ate either the tail or head of any vertebrate animal, the head of the unborn child would become large and his or her extremities weak. Eating the entrails of animals or fish was thought to cause the cord to wind dangerously around the baby. Since seagull eggs are marked with freckles, a mother would not consume these if she wanted the child's skin to be clear. In addition, porcupine meat reportedly would cause the baby to have a stuffy nose as well as to be clumsy, clubfooted, or pigeon-toed (Hildebrand 41).

Most influences described in the existing literature have a direct bearing on the nutritional wellbeing and health of Indigenous women and their children. An increasing dependence on less nutritionally dense marketed foods and a more sedentary lifestyle have resulted in rising rates of malnutrition, along with noncommunicable conditions such as obesity and type 2 diabetes, particularly among women (Egeland et al. 380; Kuhnlein et al. 1451; Neufeld, "We Practically Lived" 28). Food insecurity is also a serious concern for many Indigenous communities (Power 95; Willows et al. 1152). Dietary behaviours in pregnancy are, however, changeable and influenced by a variety of factors not well understood. Little research has explored the potential effects of these many variables, particularly how they may influence the nutritional status and long-term health of Indigenous women and their children for generations to come.

METHODOLOGY

Explorative qualitative research methods were used for this study. Semistructured and unstructured interviews took place with a generational sample of twenty-six mothers and grandmothers, beginning in June and continuing until thirty-five interviews were completed in October 2001. Following the completion and review of the initial interviews, more focused unstructured interviews took place with key informants. Two grandmothers and four mothers were interviewed for a second time. Select topics became the focus of these subsequent conversations. For the grandmothers, topics included the following: prenatal food avoidances; dietary factors associated with diabetes onset; baby size; generational lifestyle differences; diabetes symptoms; traditional medicines, and dietary consequences for mother and child. Mothers provided details about wild meat consumption during pregnancy; maternal health effects of environmental contaminants; food cravings; health properties of foods; maternal dietary taboos; baby size; and solutions for local food insecurity.

MOTHERS AND GRANDMOTHERS

Theoretical sampling was used to recruit participants of differing ages, backgrounds, experiences, and beliefs. The sample of women was selected from long-term female residents. Half of the women were of childbearing age and will be referred to as mothers. The second group of women were all recognized as grandmothers in the community. All of the women had given birth to at least one child and lived locally. The women selected to participate as grandmothers and mothers were not members of the same family. The overall sample size for the investigation was twenty-eight; fourteen grandmothers and fourteen mothers participated. Grandmothers ranged in age from fifty-nine to eighty-seven years, with a median age of 71.4. Mothers ranged in age from eighteen years to thirty-six years of age, with a median age of 26.8.

The number of pregnancies ranged from three to thirteen for the older women; however, the median number of babies born was eight. Most (64 percent) of the grandmothers visited a doctor frequently for prenatal care during their childbearing years. Only one older woman talked about seeing a midwife during her pregnancies. Two grandmothers chose not to receive prenatal care prior to their deliveries and delivered at home. The number of pregnancies reported by the group of mothers ranged from one to seven with a median of three births for each woman. Four of the women were pregnant at the time of the interview. The other ten women participating had all recently given birth, one woman to twins. All of the mothers interviewed stated that they made regular monthly visits to a local hospital physician. A large proportion of these women, 43 percent, had attended prenatal classes at the local health centre.

ANALYSIS

Each interview was transcribed verbatim and reviewed for descriptive themes before proceeding to secondary interviews. Themes and categories emerging from the transcripts and field notes were initially coded manually for further analysis. At the time, NUD*IST 4.0 software was used to organize, browse, search, code, categorize, and interpret the interview text. The constant comparative method of data analysis associated with grounded theory was employed to assist in pattern identification. Identified events were compared with events and other categories to identify relationships (Morse and Field 140). The intent of grounded theory moves beyond description to allow for a more unified explanation of processes or actions (Corbin and Strauss 87). As subsequent interviews were conducted and coded, categories became more descriptive and relationships and outliers more apparent. Typical events as well as behaviours and perceptions at this point were summarized.

ETHICAL CONSIDERATIONS

Prior to making the first visit to the research community, I contacted the Chief and Band Council in writing to seek approval for the research study. The Band Councillor responsible for health care in the community signed a letter of permission. Copies of these documents were sent to the Health Information and Research (HIR)

Committee with the Assembly of Manitoba Chiefs. The Health Research Ethics Board at the University of Manitoba approved the research proposal. Both formal and informal committees were established with health authorities and interested community members. Meetings took place with local agencies and health centre staff in the community to obtain input and feedback on research goals and objectives. Health authorities in the area formally reviewed the interview guide. Women provided their informed consent before participating in the study. Pseudonyms have been used to protect the identity of the participants. Names beginning with the letter "M" refer to mothers and "G" to grandmothers.

RESULTS

Georgia: Well, I worked hard. I never stayed in bed until ten o'clock. I ate all the food that was before me, that was off the land. I never knew anything about junk food then. Never had no fried foods. Always was boiled or baked. That's how I grew up.

Maya: I stay away from foods that are no good for me that I like more. I found that out. Cut down on my salt and sugar intake. 'Cause I, before I was pregnant, my husband was getting after me for drinking too much Pepsi.

All of the participants were asked how they changed their eating patterns during past pregnancies. Each provided examples of foods that were unavailable or prohibited during pregnancy. In addition, they named specific foods they felt had an influence on fetal health. These topics were then further developed during four of the six unstructured secondary interviews. Both mothers and grandmothers described maternal dietary practices that reflected societal, cultural, and familial teachings. Eating patterns were often altered during pregnancy based on advice received from female family members, friends as well as from health care professionals and para-professionals. These teachings were expressed either in the form of suggestions, recommendations, or advice relating to foods and other dietary practices.

MATERNAL ADVICE

Both mothers and grandmothers talked about what foods they felt were of most benefit to the health of mother and child. They mentioned fruits and vegetables as well as milk. Mothers had the most to say about the advantages of consuming cow's milk or milk products. When women were asked to give examples of foods they would eat for the health of their baby, all but one mother mentioned milk. Even women who were lactose intolerant prepregnancy drank milk while carrying their children. Marcy said, "when I was pregnant for some reason it ... [didn't bother me] at all. Like I just love it now. I didn't have to take Lactade at all." If milk was not enjoyable to some mothers, they still felt they should be drinking it. As Martha commented, "I forced myself to drink milk." Michelle talked directly about the health benefits of consuming milk while pregnant: "Just like they told me, like they gave me those pamphlets ... like it affects the brain, her bones ... like milk and I drink a lot of that too." Margaret explained she drank milk because she "heard it was good for the baby, and for the baby's bones and ... for my bones too."

Six grandmothers talked about the benefits of milk consumption when asked what foods they felt helped the baby they were carrying. More commonly, however, they talked about the health benefits of fresh fruit and vegetables. Giselle, described her grandmother's advice to "eat a lot of fruit and vegetables" during her pregnancies. Nine others had similar advice. Gretel's mother told her that when she was pregnant all she had to live from was "garden stuff" which was "the best foods for ya." Similarly, Geraldine talked about the benefits of having a garden and access to fresh vegetables: "I always liked vegetables. Even my girls are having children I always had a garden, you know, and offer them all these things to cook. I tell 'em cook them. They're healthy for you and your baby'll be okay. Some of them stayed with me when they were pregnant, so what I ate out of the gardens and that I would make them eat."

Grandmothers also had advice on the preparation of foods. Five older women felt that boiling or roasting fresh foods was healthier than using oil to fry foods. Gail explained, "I think that's why there's so many sick.... not cooking and boiling stuff you know. Too much fried." Gina echoed these concerns:

> I think that just what goes into you goes into the baby too, and I think it's best to be careful. To think of the baby first before you think of your own taste buds and just have the things that are nutritional. Even though it's faster, you know, to fry something up than it is to take time to boil it or roast it or do it in more healthful, nutritional ways. Especially when you have a lot of little children around you; they're hungry too and waiting for something to be served to them and it's just so easy to get the old frying pan out.

Advice in the form of dietary opinions and lifestyle recommendations was shared from women in both age categories. Grandmothers understood pregnancy as a "normal" event, which did not hinder rigorous work schedules or necessarily require medical intervention. When asked what they recalled most about previous pregnancies, for example, Geraldine replied in the following way:

> Eating good foods. Feeding them good anyway. Yeah, I always ate good, and I worked hard. I worked with all my children. I picked potatoes and picked carrots, onions. We worked on farms. We dug Seneca root. We never laid around. We'd get up early in the morning and do our work and everything because the Elders said you're not supposed to sleep long. You get up and work. Move around!

The only comments that these grandmothers made about sickness focused on childbirth instead of the pregnancy itself. Gwen remembered "being sick" while in labour. She went on to say that "the other parts I didn't mind, being [pregnant] ... you know, when you're carrying. I worked right till the end. Never laid around or sat around, you know." Gwen also compared her experiences with the younger women in the community: "You see some of the young girls now. They gotta sleep, they gotta rest, you know, and we didn't then. We did all our own housework. Nobody came in and did any work for us I mean."

All but one grandmother talked about a collective work ethic when they were pregnant, in tandem with concerns about the changing lifestyle of young mothers in the community. Giselle had a lot to say on the topic, particularly related to the size of babies and the activity levels promoted by her grandmother:

> She really wanted me to be active because I find that if you were active enough and not laze around, your baby never did really get so big. Today they have babies ten pounds and even more. I never had a baby like that. And I can't remember, you know, I used to walk a lot and never exercised, but walking and doing all the housework and stuff. I guess that was pretty good, yeah. So that kind of kept the weight of the baby down.

Gina received similar advice from her grandmother: "Get out of bed in the morning. Don't just lay there. Like put your feet on the floor and stand up as soon as you wake up." She went on to also explain her grandmother's rational:

> It prevented, it helped the baby stay well in the womb. She felt it did a lot of prevention with her. Women that didn't.... they were tired all the time; they laid around a lot. Their babies were not so healthy as the people that were active. I think a lot of it goes through the blood, and if you're active, more oxygen going into your blood more, more oxygen will get to the baby. Keep the baby healthy.

DIETARY PROSCRIPTIONS

Ten grandmothers and eleven mothers spoke about specific foods or dietary practices they were taught to avoid when pregnant. Although not as many women talked about discouraged practices compared to cravings or aversions they may have experienced, food categories were similar. Mothers mentioned fourteen different items or practices they were encouraged to avoid. Those most frequently cited included Pepsi, fried foods, vegetables, meat, alcohol, sweets, tea, salt, lard, and smoking. Grandmothers noted thirteen similar categories, with the exception of canned foods.

Many mothers talked about being told specifically not to drink Pepsi. Marcy described how her family and friends made her feel if she had any Pepsi while pregnant: "If I had Pepsi, everyone would be like, 'don't drink that'! Make me feel real guilty and with my last two, my husband would only let me have one a day." Mabel talked about feeling similar pressure from her doctor while attending prenatal visits at the local hospital:

> He explained to me, when a woman goes into labour and kids come out and they're screaming or upset or whatever ... the same way they react when there's drugs in their system or they're FAS [Fetal Alcohol Syndrome]. He said that these babies come out addicted to something they don't know what it is. Because people aren't honest when they're asked all of these questions. So I ended up telling him, well I drink a two-litre Pepsi a day. He said that makes a big difference. He said they're going to come out and want caffeine. He said that's what makes them upset the first few days.

Mothers grouped Pepsi into the larger category of junk food to be avoided during pregnancy. Carbonated and sweetened beverages, as well as other caffeinated beverages, potato chips, and other "treats" were grouped into the same category. When asked what things she was told to abstain from, Matilda immediately stated, "junk food," which she went on to describe as the following: "pop, coffee. That's it, mostly that. Junk food, coffee, caffeine. Told not to eat stuff like that with caffeine in there." Both groups of women also talked about the effects and health outcomes of Pepsi consumption. Three mothers and one grandmother made comments about the sugar content of Pepsi as well as the salt content of other junk food, and their effects on the health of the mother and baby. For example, Mary talked about the adverse effects of sugar and salt: "Well, if you don't eat right you're going to maybe get diabetes or high blood pressure and stuff like that. Mostly I stay away from like salty foods 'cause can make you have high blood pressure. I try and stay away from like salty foods like chips and stuff like that. And, like for me, I don't drink pop."

Georgia alluded to the adverse effects of junk food, such as Pepsi, on the health of the developing child: "I think that's why today there's so much hyper children … too much sugars and junk. Learning disabilities they have now." Two other grandmothers and three mothers also responded with comments related to the physical health and wellbeing of the baby. Giselle said that "carbonated pop" was something her grandmother told her to stay away from. She explained that such "gassy" foods will "give the baby cramps, it will give you cramps, you know." She also grouped pop into the sweets category, which included items such as cakes and chocolate.

Three grandmothers and one mother talked about the negative effects of certain vegetables they were advised against consuming while pregnant. For example, Giselle's grandmother cautioned against eating "acidy" foods, which she described as something that "will give me gas, or give the baby cramps." She was, therefore, discouraged from eating a variety of vegetables such as turnips, cucumber, cabbage, or cauliflower. Eggs were allowed only infrequently for similar reasons. Women were also told to avoid spicy foods. Marion reported craving hot peppers during one pregnancy, and her mother advised her against eating them because they might "burn your baby." Gina described at more length the unfavourable effects of spicy foods on the baby: "Well, it takes your body more time to digest those kinds of things so it makes you tend to want to be more, you know, you want to sit around or lay around while those things are passing through you. Whereas if you are having more nutritional foods like a regular hamburger compared to those spicy taco things, that will give you more instant energy."

Of all the younger women, only Maya talked about, as she referred to it, "wives' tales" or stories that restrict certain foods during pregnancy. She remembered three distinct food categories that her mother, grandmother, and aunties had warned her about eating when pregnant. The first was a proscription against the consumption of strawberries, blueberries, and beets. These brightly pigmented foods were believed to cause the baby to be born with, "strawberry marks or blueberry marks on the skin." Maya also talked about eggs, meat, and lard:

The older ladies will say don't eat too much eggs because your baby will drool too much when they're born. After they're born, they'll be messy babies, like they'll drool. Just after the baby's born, not to eat any meat 'cause you'll clot your blood or something. Don't eat any meat, anything too solid ... what she said about lard, the baby will have some kind of difficulty when it came down to labour. It was harder to push out the baby. Like [the lard] made the baby kind of sticky sort of thing, like it was harder for the woman.

WEIGHT GAIN

All participants shared personal experiences along with recommendations they had received concerning maternal weight and fetal size. Grandmothers had the most to say on this topic and were worried about the amount of weight young women in the community gained when pregnant. Gretel was especially alarmed: "I see that some of them are pregnant, the ones I see, they lay in bed and order chicken.... laying in bed! I see them there. When are you having your baby? End of November? Oh, holy heck! Think they have an elephant. Yeah, I think it's what they eat, but they should be careful what they eat."

Only the grandmothers discussed the regulation of food during pregnancy, mainly in relation to the eventual size of the baby and possible difficulty during delivery. Six grandmothers talked about being encouraged to watch their overall intake. Gloria remembered her own mother's guidance: "my mother would tell me not to eat too much. Just eat sometime again. Don't eat it all the same time." According to Giselle, she was told by her mother to "eat moderate. Like don't go overfill yourself. Know when to stop." Her mother's rationale was "your baby will be too big if you do those things, and you'll have a real hard time to have the baby."

Grandmothers also talked specifically about certain foods that were discouraged during pregnancy to reduce the baby's size. Gladys recalled that "the old grandparents used to tell us not to eat too much meat because they said it made the baby too big, too much weight and it would be a harder delivery." Bannock was another food that was not eaten in large quantity to keep the size and weight of the baby down. Geraldine described her grandmother's advice to consume foods, such as fresh fruit, so she would not be "gaining all this weight." Gwen spoke about the cumulative amount of weight she was allowed to gain while pregnant: "You just watched your diet, like you didn't put on too much weight and then we didn't. I wasn't heavy then." Others talked specifically about the size and proportions of the fetus. For example, Grace was told by her grandparents that if a pregnant woman slept too long "the baby's head grew and not the body."

Nine of the thirteen young women spoke about maternal and fetal weight, several about the attempts to lose weight or the difficulties losing weight. Marion was "cautious" about her diet while pregnant because of her experience with her first daughter: "I didn't want to gain as much weight with her because it's hard to lose. So I tried not to eat not to eat 'til I was full. I tried to stop before I got full. Tried to control how much I eat." Megan regretted the weight she gained with her first pregnancy because she was 140 pounds before she got pregnant and then shot to 220 pounds. She had difficulty losing the weight postpartum. Both Megan and Marion explained that their weight control efforts were out of concern for their babies' health. Marion recalled advice she received from a nurse: "she said that the food that I eat like the fat foods, like McDonald's, will make my baby fat, and I'll have a hard time to deliver. I didn't know that. Didn't know that she could [be] overweight." Her first pregnancy she delivered a daughter, who was almost ten pounds. The delivery was a difficult one and resulted in the baby's collarbone being broken "because she was so big."

Marcy talked extensively about baby size and maternal weight gain. She discussed the weight of her peers and described her experiences in the community and the peer pressure she felt about her own children:

A lot of girls, especially the younger ones nowadays, like I'll take my girls to the hospital and they say, 'oh your kids are so tiny, they're so small.' And they'll say it like it's insulting, like is your girl ever skinny. Especially her, they call her a bony baby. So they're bigger and the fatter they are they think it's more healthier. They think like I take care of my kid better or something like that.

DISCUSSION

Although the findings described in this chapter are undoubtedly reflective of the somewhat exploratory nature of this study, some interesting patterns and responses did indeed emerge and warrant discussion. Maternal dietary and lifestyle patterns had changed considerably between the two generations of women at the time of these interviews. Grandmothers emphasized their concerns for the long-term health of mothers and their children in the community. Specific types and quantities of foods and decreased activity patterns were identified as leading to excessive prenatal weight gain and difficult deliveries. Both mothers and grandmothers associated fresh foods, such as fruits, vegetables and milk, with healthy pregnancy outcomes. Proscribed foods and beverages were also similar between generations. Junk food, and greasy and spicy food were viewed as being most harmful.

Similar advice in the form of dietary and behavioural prescriptions and proscriptions has been previously reported in the literature. Carole Hildebrand and Elizabeth Sokoloski discuss the nutritional value and adequacy of maternal diets in Minnesota and Manitoba, respectively. The results from Sokoloski's study with First Nations women share some likeness to comments made by the group of grandmothers from Peguis: "a well-balanced diet and moderate portions are believed to help maintain a healthy pregnancy" and "exercise in moderation is believed to be a healthy practice" (95). In Minnesota during the 1970s, Indigenous women were similarly encouraged to "do hard work" while pregnant (Hildebrand 36). Women reported that if they remained very active the child would be "loosened," which made the delivery easier. Eating healthily and not sleeping excessively during the second and third trimester were also associated with preventing difficult delivery (Neander and Morse 192). Inactivity during pregnancy could cause a difficult labour, a large baby, and for the baby to be unhealthy, lazy and "stuck to one part of the body and womb" (Clarke 28). The *Nutritional Newsletter* published in 1982 by Health and Welfare

Canada included elements of similar prenatal customs and practices. In Saskatchewan, First Nation women were encouraged to work and exercise to decrease the size of the fetus. In British Columbia walking was encouraged and getting up early in the morning, which "helped the baby move around and it wouldn't stay in one place when it was time for birth" (Canada 19). In more recent Canadian studies, healthy eating has meant consuming vegetables, fruits and avoiding fast foods (Vallianatos et al. 115) and other foods with high fat content (O'Driscoll et al. 26). First Nations women in Québec and northwestern Ontario also expressed the view that exercise during pregnancy was important not only for maternal health but for an easier labour and birth.

Grandmothers in Peguis spoke about the regulation of food quantity during pregnancy—discouraging the consumption of foods such as meat and bannock to keep the weight of the baby down. In a number of other North American Indigenous communities, food was somewhat restricted during the latter part of pregnancy to prevent problems during labour and delivery. In Washington State, women were encouraged to eat less near term and walk frequently to ensure a smaller baby and, thus, a less traumatic delivery (Bushnell 257). Participants in the Minnesota study were not to eat a lot any time during pregnancy, but particularly immediately prior to birth (Hildebrand 37). Hildebrand and Clarke describe food restrictions based on their potential "marking" on the unborn child. Clarke notes that crab was prohibited for consumption during pregnancy because the its physical characteristics could cause the baby to grow up with "bow legs" and soft bones. As one of the mothers from Peguis described, strawberries were prohibited for the red skin marks they may make on the child.

Other dietary proscriptions described by women in Peguis, such as mothers being discouraged from consuming junk food and spicy or greasy foods, do not appear to be reported elsewhere. The majority of the taboos or restrictions relate to appropriate weight gain and size of the fetus. Factors impacting a child's entrance into the world seem to influence maternal advice most. The rationale and reasoning behind many of these ideologies, proscriptions, and prescriptions also deserve reflection. There is scant amount of published interpretation, however, as to the implications of gestational dietary behaviours. Early articles suggest that perhaps many may have originated as public health measures against disease or foods with certain toxic properties. A study in East Africa also proposed that the observance of taboos by pregnant women could relate to totem observance (Trant 703). A mother and grandmother in Peguis made the association with animals that were restricted for their personal consumption. Another author has suggested that food proscriptions are observed to prevent nausea and discomfort (Rao 96). Certain nutritious foods were instinctively selected by women during their pregnancies to enrich the overall diet (Rao 96). Clarke acknowledges the presence of such beliefs. For the Coast Salish women in her study, if a woman "listened" to her body, she could learn what was harmful or beneficial to her health and her baby's health (29).

Regardless of the variety of hypotheses and explanations put forward, the patterns of beliefs regarding prenatal dietary practices are obviously complex. As Paul Fieldhouse has stated, "the interrelationships of food habits with other elements of cultural behaviour and with environmental forces emphasizes the futility of treating food choices as being intellectual decisions made on rational nutritional grounds alone" (35). Others have explained that for many Indigenous women pregnancy is viewed as a normal and a natural event requiring no medical intervention (Loughlin; Bushnell; Sokoloski). Bernice Loughlin has found that Navajo women questioned the need for prenatal care when an expectant mother continued with her usual lifestyle and dietary habits. These sentiments were certainly echoed by the older women in Peguis, whereas the younger women tended to have a more medicalized view of pregnancy.

These dietary and behavioural prescriptions as well as proscriptions described by both generations of women in this study provide insight into mechanisms through which prenatal health information has historically been disseminated in the community. The advice the group of grandmothers received as young women is not entirely different from the prescriptions described by the young mothers. Both groups indicated the importance of consuming local and nutrient-dense foods during pregnancy for the optimal health of mother and child. The grandmothers tended to emphasize fresh foods from the land and were careful not to gain too much weight to ensure an infant's safe arrival. They were encouraged by their mothers and grandmothers to keep active. Responses from the younger participants, though similar to their Elders, seemed to be associated with medical advice or formal nutrition education messages. Pressure was felt from peers and medical professionals to decrease the consumption of processed or junk food. For the younger generation, prenatal health education and teachings may therefore be assumed to have originated from health professionals, instead of more informal familial contacts.

The group of mothers may therefore be equipped with what Clarke refers to as more contemporary teachings. Maternal advice or direction from their own mothers or grandmothers was noticeably absent in the interviews. In Clarke's study, these more traditional or historically embedded teachings about "emotions and spirituality" were associated with higher levels of commitment and behavioural modifications (26). The major sources of such teachings and knowledge were found to be mothers, mothers-in-laws and grandmothers, during all stages of pregnancy. The community emphasized the modification of a woman's daily living patterns while carrying her child. Instead of restrictions, additions in the form of prescriptions, such as increased and regular activity patterns, were taught (Clarke 26). These forms of traditional knowledge or Indigenous knowledge have been defined as "practical common sense, based on teachings and experiences passed on from generation to generation," or simply "a way of life" (Cochran and Geller 1405).

Certainly a complex and unique set of influences on food practices exists for Indigenous women and communities. Food choice and eating practices are influenced by social relationships and cultural membership in tight knit and often remote locations (Omura 153). Food serves as a strong symbolic social resource to link family relationships in the present and past (Thompson et al. 733). The practice of redefining foods and practices categorized as "unhealthy" by the medical establishment may improve the health of future generations; however, these notions of education risk further disrupting people and relationships from the past. Frustration and the rejection of prenatal care and nutrition counselling may also signal a lack of connection between messages delivered and the evolving worldview of Indigenous mothers. Taking a community-based approach toward prenatal nutrition that includes Elder women will not only increase the use of care during pregnancy but empower Indigenous women during this revered and celebrated period of the lifecycle.

WORKS CITED

Bushnell, Jeanette M. "Northwest Coast American Indians' Beliefs about Childbirth." *Issues in Health Care of Women*, vol. 3, no. 4, 1981, pp. 249-61.

Canada, Medical Services Branch. *Nutritional Newsletter.* National Health and Welfare, 1982.

Clarke, H. F. "Childbearing Practices of Coast Salish Indians in British Columbia: An Ethnographic Study." *Through the Looking Glass: Children and Health Promotion*, edited by Jane Ross and Vangie Bergum, Canadian Public Health Association, 1990, pp. 21-34.

Cochran, Patricia L., and Alyson L. Geller. "The Melting Ice Cellar: What Native Traditional Knowledge Is Teaching Us about Global Warming and Environmental Change." *American Journal of Public Health*, vol. 92, no. 9, 2002, pp. 1404-9.

Corbin, Juliet, and Anselm Strauss. *Basics of Qualitative Research: Techniques and Procedures for Developing Grounded Theory.* 3rd ed., Sage Publications, 2008.

Egeland, Grace M., et al. "Traditional Food and Monetary Access to Market-food: Correlates of Food Insecurity among Inuit Preschoolers." *International Journal of Circumpolar Health*, vol. 70, no. 4, 2011, pp. 373-83.

Fieldhouse, Paul. *Food and Nutrition: Customs and Culture.* Croom Helm, 1986.

Giroux, Isabelle, et al. "Weight History of Overweight Pregnant Women." *Canadian Journal of Dietetic Practice and Research*, vol. 70, no. 3, 2009, pp. 127-34.

Hildebrand, Carol E. "Maternal-Child Care among the Chippewa: A Study of the Past and Present." *Military Medicine*, vol. 135, 1970, pp. 35-43.

Kuhnlein, Harriet V., et al. "Arctic Indigenous Peoples Experience the Nutrition Transition with Changing Dietary Patterns and Obesity." *Journal of Nutrition,* vol. 134, no. 6, 2004, pp. 1447-53.

Loughlin, Bernice W. "Pregnancy in the Navajo Culture." *Nursing Outlook,* vol. 13, 1965, pp. 55-8.

Moffatt, Michael E. K. "Nutritional Problems of Native Canadian Mothers and Children." *Canadian Family Physician,* vol. 35, 1989, pp. 377-82.

Morse, Janice M., and Peggy Anne Field. *Qualitative Research Methods for Health Professionals.* Sage Publications, 1995.

Murcott, Anne, editor. *The Sociology of Food and Eating.* Gower, 1983.

Neander, Wendy L., and Janice M. Morse. "Tradition and Change in the Northern Alberta Woodlands Cree: Implications for Infant Feeding Practice." *Canadian Journal of Public Health,* vol. 80, no. 3, 1989, pp. 190-94.

Neufeld, Hannah T. "Food Perceptions and Concerns of Aboriginal Women Coping with Gestational Diabetes in Winnipeg, Manitoba." *Journal of Nutrition Education and Behavior,* vol. 43, no. 6, 2011, pp. 482-91.

Neufeld, Hannah T. *Prenatal Dietary Reflections among Two Generations in a Southern First Nations Community.* MSc thesis, University of Manitoba, 2003.

Neufeld, Hannah T. "We Practically Lived Off the Land: Generational Changes in Food Acquisition Patterns among First Nations Mothers and Grandmothers." *Mothers of the Nations: Indigenous Mothering as Global Resistance, Reclaiming and Recovery,* edited by D. Memee Lavell-Harvard and Kim Anderson, Demeter Press, 2014, pp. 27-45.

O'Driscoll, Terry, et al. "Traditional First Nations Birthing Practices: Interviews with Elders in Northwestern Ontario." *Journal of Obstetrics and Gynaecology Canada,* vol. 33, no. 1, 2011, pp. 24-29.

Omura, Emily. "Mino-Miijim's 'Good Food for the Future': Beyond Culturally Appropriate Diabetes Programs." *Indigenous Peoples and Diabetes: Community Empowerment and Wellness,* edited by Mariana K. Leal Ferreira and Gretchen Chesley Lang, Carolina Academic Press, 2006, pp. 139-65.

Power, Elaine. M. "Conceptualizing Food Security for Aboriginal

People in Canada." *Canadian Journal of Public Health,* vol. 99, no. 2, 2008, pp. 95-7.

QSR International. *NVivo Qualitative Data Analysis Software.* QSR International, www. qsrinternational.com/. Accessed 24 Aug. 2017.

Rao, Meera. "Food Beliefs of Rural Women during the Reproductive Years in Dharwad, India." *Ecology of Food and Nutrition,* vol. 16, no. 2, 1985, pp. 93-103.

Sanjur, Diva. *Social and Cultural Perspectives in Nutrition.* Prentice-Hall, 1982.

Schaefer, Sara E., et al. "Sources of Food Affect Dietary Adequacy of Inuit Women of Childbearing Age in Arctic Canada." *Journal of Health, Population and Nutrition,* vol. 29, no. 5, 2011, pp. 454-64.

Sokoloski, Elizabeth H. "Canadian First Nations Women's Beliefs about Pregnancy and Prenatal Care." *Canadian Journal of Nursing Research,* vol. 27, no. 1, 1995, pp. 89-100.

Trant, Hope. "Food Taboos in East Africa." *The Lancet,* vol. 264, no. 6840, 1954, pp. 703-5.

Thompson, Samantha, et al. "The Social and Cultural Context of Risk and Prevention: Food and Physical Activity in an Urban Aboriginal Community." *Health Education & Behavior,* vol. 27, no. 6, 2000, pp. 725-43.

Vallianatos, Helen, et al. "Beliefs and Practices of First Nation Women about Weight Gain during Pregnancy and Lactation: Implications for Women's Health." *CJNR,* vol. 38, no. 1, 2006, pp. 102-19.

Willows, Noreen, et al. "Prevalence and Sociodemographic Risk Factors Related to Household Food Security in Aboriginal Peoples in Canada." *Public Health Nutrition,* vol. 12, no. 8, 2009, pp. 1150-6.

3.

Culture, Identity, and Spirituality in American Indians and Native People of Alaska Pregnancy Campaigns

TERRY L. RENTNER, DINAH A. TETTEH, AND LYNDA DIXON

I *SHARE INSIGHTS on health and Indian identity from the knowledge, perspective, and lived experiences as a Cherokee woman and citizen of the Cherokee Nation and a co-author of this chapter. During years of receiving healthcare for my children and me through federal government programs, I was often in the waiting room for healthcare. Together with other Indigenous groups, we waited and waited, surrounded by bold signs threatening the loss of our healthcare if specific rules were broken, including being late. We waited, but we were forbidden to keep our health providers waiting. In that space and in the examination rooms, we were treated with insensitivity to cultural expectations and with disrespect in both verbal and nonverbal communication acts. One on occasion, I was there when a young pregnant Indian woman tried several times to get the receptionist to allow her in an examination room because she was in labour. For four hours, she waited while occasionally, and politely, asking for help. None of the staff or the healthcare providers waited on her. After many hours, she gave birth on the floor of that room of waiting. Rather than treating her and the baby with kindness and dignity, staff and medical personnel muttered about the mess, one nurse asked tersely, "Why didn't you tell us that you were in labour?" I thought, "Why didn't anyone tell us how we would be treated?" (Dixon, "Interactions").*

The story of the labouring woman, her heart and her body on the ground, gives insight to the abundant problems of a government bureaucracy operated by non-Indian management and healthcare providers (Dixon, "Cherokee"; Dixon and Shaver) and the lack of an ethics of care by some health practitioners who are not sensitive to the history, diversity, culture, identity of Nations (G. Hanson 247). This story of waiting and birthing is one of many that illustrate the ongoing harmful effects of colonialism on the Cherokee Nation and other Nations, particularly in the area of health and wellbeing. In this study, we focus on one health concern—safe and healthy pregnancies—but this work could apply to any number of health and wellbeing concerns for American Indians.

This chapter explores the need for sensitivity to cultural nuances, identity, and spirituality in safe and healthy pregnancy campaigns among American Indians and Native People of Alaska (AI/AN). These terms are used interchangeably and together and refer to individuals who self-identify as either American Indian or Alaska Native. Cultural identity aspects—including class, age, gender, and sexual orientation—are often ignored in health campaigns aimed at Indigenous peoples, such as those of the American Indian and Alaska Natives, who suffer from a far worse status of health than most other persons within the U.S. and Canada (Brown et al.; Rentner et al.; Turpel). Researchers suggest health prevention campaigns must be attentive to history, traditional practices, and spirituality (Holmes and Antell; Rentner and Lengel; Stone et al.; Whitbeck et al.), and interventions should give the participants the skills so they are not damaged by discrimination, historical and cultural loss, and forced assimilation.

PREGNANCY RATES AND RISK FACTORS

Although teen pregnancy rates among ages fifteen to nineteen have declined over the past two decades, the pregnancy rate among American Indian and Alaska Natives girls are alarmingly high compared to non-Hispanic whites (thirty-one births per one thousand compared to ten births per one thousand) (Wiltz 3). Just as alarming is the 2006 study that found a 50 percent infant mortality rate among AI/ AN compared to non-Hispanic whites ("Looking to the Past" 8). Many of the negative health consequences contributing to infant mortality are preventable through proper prenatal care (J. Hanson 29). Higher rates of hypertension, obesity, diabetes, smoking, and alcohol use occur more often among American Indian and American Natives during pregnancy than other groups (Alexander et al. 5). For example, approximately 18 percent of Indigenous women in the U.S. smoked during pregnancy as compared to 14 percent of non-Hispanic white women (Indian Health Service 9). The percentage of babies with fetal alcohol syndrome diagnosed at birth per 10,000 births is 29.9 for American Indians compared to 0.09 among Euro-Americans; 0.3 among Asians; 0.8 among Hispanics; and 6.0 among African Americans (National Institute on Alcohol Abuse and Alcoholism).

Access to prenatal care is one factor attributed to high mortality rates. Claudia Long and Mary Ann Curry describe a conflict between traditional beliefs and practices and the Western model of care as a major barrier to proper prenatal care (205). The authors also cite both provider characteristics, such as disrespect, hostility, and paternalism, along with personal barriers, such as fear and bad experiences with healthcare providers, as contributors to poor prenatal care. Cultural beliefs may also increase risk factors for pregnancy and delivery. For example, as recently as 1944, it was not uncommon for Alaska Native women to go into the wilderness to give birth (Dillard and Olrun-Volkheimer 64). Even today, pregnant Alaska Native women are considered spoiled by modern technology because they have access to epidurals, pain medication, and Caesarean sections that other Indigenous women lack (65).

WHOSE VOICE IS IT?

Health campaigns are typically designed to create awareness, to increase knowledge, and to change attitudes and behaviours. In designing campaigns, communication practitioners should first question the underlying motives of a health campaign and whether the campaign is serving the institutions of power or the populations of which they claim to serve. Just by their very nature, campaigns "necessarily compromise certain values and interests, often individual freedoms, in order to promote values and interests deemed more socially, economically, or morally compelling by the organization sponsoring the change effort" (Salmon 20). The development of campaigns in which the voices of the intended population are not represented could arguably be perceived as representing institutions of power. Patricia Curtin and Kenn Gaither would assert that campaigns must represent the "standpoint of the other" (1) and must take into account "diverse cultural values, the role of relative power in relationships, and fluid, often conflicting identities" ("Contested" 3).

Researchers have noted that unsuccessful health campaigns aimed at Native audiences most often do not involve American Indians in key roles in the development and implementation of such campaigns (Rentner et al. 15), and many focused on changing individual behaviours. This has historically been a problem when campaign messages are missing the mark. Take the campaign on early breast cancer detection among Chinese Americans, who were more likely to have undetected breast cancer because "existing early-detection messages did not address cultural values or particular concerns" about their susceptibility for getting breast cancer (Guttman and Solmon 536). Consider the campaign for foot care to older Ethiopians showing an older man having his feet washed by woman. Although this portrayal resonated with older women as culturally appropriate, younger Ethiopian women argued it reinforces traditional gender role that must be changed (532).

Campaigns focusing on individual behaviours can be both beneficial and harmful. For example, a weight loss campaign may provide individuals with the "tools" to change their behaviour, such as planned exercise and healthy eating choices. Failure to change these behaviours may be viewed as laziness or irresponsibility, and the individual is then labelled as a burden to family and society (Guttman and Solmon 542).

More ethical and effective messaging are the community-based campaigns where "community participants more often view an intervention as an opportunity to change the community context in support of behavior change" (Middlestadt et. al. 295). Participation becomes the norm because community members feel a sense of control and ownership of the community-based campaign. Examples of successful community-based health campaigns include the Stanford Three-Community Study, the Stanford Five-City Project, and the Minnesota Heart Health Program (Hornik; Flora et al.; Winkleby et al.). Community-based campaigns provide opportunities for voices of the intended target audience to be heard. These include messages that will and will not work. For example, in healthy and safe pregnancy campaigns, planners need to recognize the conflict between the Western model of care and the barriers faced by AI/AN—including fears of medical providers and procedures, prior negative experiences with the health system, and the belief in what Long and Curry refer to as the "naturalness of pregnancy" (206). They further assert how prenatal care among this population should be flipped from the Western model: Tribal Elders, grandmothers, and others in collaboration with doctors should provide the majority of care. Analysis of successful AI/AN safe and healthy pregnancy campaigns described later illustrates the importance of community-based campaigns that consider the roles of history, culture, identity, and spirituality as essential components.

HEALTH COMMUNICATION CAMPAIGNS AND THE OTHER

Dominant cultures that impose their culturally appropriate strategies in health communication campaigns are highly problematic. Douglas Kellner describes how the role of Other is created from "boundaries and borders of class, gender, race, sexuality, and the other constituents that differentiate individuals from each other and through which people construct their identities" (12). Curtin and Gaither argue that identities are often defined through difference and warn of the "inherent dangers of cultural stereotyping and forming unidimensional portraits of 'the other'" ("Privileging" 103). They further point out that because identities are comprised of a multitude of socially constructed meanings and practices, such as class, ethnicity, nationality, and gender, they are in flux and fragmented ("Privileging" 101). Thus, the Self represents the dominant culture, and the Other is seen as the "unspoken and invisible" among the predominantly white aesthetic and cultural discourses (Hall 114). As a result, many campaigns, while having good intentions, have actually deepened the boundaries and borders of difference, mainly through lack of understanding of the role that culture, power, and identity play in campaign communication practice (Curtin and Gaither, "Privileging" 106).

The divide between Self and Other becomes clear when examining the relationship of spirituality and health. One such example can be found in a study of 148 Native male and female adolescents through the use of twenty focus groups (Garwick et al.). One of the main themes emerging from this study of Native youth is the need to include family members and Elders in discussion and activities emphasizing Native ceremonies and other cultural practices (86-7). Support groups, such as the talking circle and storytelling approaches, can help patients discuss issues, explain behaviour, and learn how to change behaviorus; they have been used as a successful and culturally appropriate intervention strategy (Hodge and Nandy). Storytelling is a communication tool used to preserve traditions of the culture. Also critical to success is the acknowledgment of the different religious practices among the many Nations.

The divide between Self and Other can be seen in the relationship between patient and physician. Hierarchies of power and ethical and equitable relationships between health and medical organizations and their targeted audiences are informed by Habermas's discourse ethics, in which dialogue must provide all parties involved equal opportunities to participate in the discourse and to challenge ideas. Those on the margins, however, rarely have an equal chance to participate in discourses surrounding mainstream health campaigns. In patient-physician visits, Native women rarely attempt to add information or answer questions thoroughly because of the actions and words of the doctors as they rush to see other patients. The obvious power distance through status of education, wealth, and culture between pregnant Native women and the usually white physician continues to constrain communication, which would lead to better outcomes. The few who tried to voice their ideas were either ignored or given a brief response, which is consistent with the disempowerment of Indigenous peoples outside the U.S. as well. In Australia, for example, Aboriginal and Torres Strait Islander peoples have been ignored in similar campaigns (Rankin). Similar findings can be found among First Nations and Métis women in Canada who were treated for gestational diabetes. In this qualitative study, researchers have found divisions of power and barriers—such as socioeconomic, attitudinal, structural, and communication—exist between the women and their healthcare providers (Neufeld 11).

OVERVIEW OF SAFE AND HEALTHY PREGNANCY CAMPAIGNS

The same failure is inherent in much of the health campaigns directed to Native audiences that do not involve American Indians in key roles in development and implementation of such campaigns. The National Campaign to Prevent Teen and Unplanned Pregnancy, for example, claims that "few programs exist to help Native youth prevent pregnancy" and further attests that none have been rigorously evaluated specifically for this target audience (Suellentrop and Hunter 4). This finding was supported in a study of thirty-one national health campaigns conducted among AI/AN by the Urban Health Institute in 2011. Only two campaigns—the Fetal Alcohol Spectrum Disorder Resource Kit and the Coming of the Blessing—are aimed at safe and healthy pregnancies ("Looking to the Past" 27, 29). Three other campaigns address the related topics of high infant death and premature birth rates, sudden infant death syndrome, and a program that encourages parents to talk to children about waiting to have sex. Twenty-one of these campaigns were created by government agencies, four were developed by philanthropic agencies such as the March of Dimes, and only five were created by Native non-profit agencies (16). Additionally, only thirteen of the thirty-one campaigns were developed specifically for the AI/AN audience (16). These staggering low numbers of health communication campaigns designed by AI/AN clearly illustrates the lack of culturally sensitive messages and further demonstrates the divide among the Self and Other. Even the better campaigns did not recognize the great diversity within all 562 Nations in the United States, a diversity is prevalent in all areas—different languages, cultures, health beliefs, and health problems.

In a Department of Health and Human Services study of evidence-based approaches to teen pregnancy prevention between 1989 and 2001, researchers found thirty-one program models with a statistically positive impact on pregnancy, sexually transmitted infections, and sexual risk behaviours, but none of these focused specifically on AI/AN groups (Goesling et al. 502). The questions raised here serve as a foundation for critiquing culturally appropriate guidelines in AI/AN health campaigns, a much understudied area. As we will explain below, multiple factors with cultural undertones, including alcohol use, contribute to the health status of AI/AN populations, and it is important that health campaigns or programs acknowledge these cultural elements for the campaigns to be effective.

Alcohol use among pregnant AI/AN populations is one of the leading contributors to unhealthy pregnancies and births, but because of the lack of agreement on methods to diagnosis fetal alcohol syndrome (FAS), both the frequency of FAS and the campaigns' successes or failures have been hard to record and disseminate. Moreover, researchers have not agreed on the number of cases of FAS because of the difficulty in diagnosis; the cultural crisis of shame for the mother, father, the child, and the extended family; and the lack of coordination among Nations and agencies (Clawson). These have hindered any meaningful evaluation of campaign success. One campaign that showed early promise was a multistrategic program implemented in Tuba City, Arizona, among the American Indian population in 1998. The rate of FAS in this city was 1.3 per 1,000 in 1982 for children younger than 15 and 2.7 per 1,000 births for children between 0 and 4 (Masis and May 485). The program used a three-pronged approach that views FAS "in a systems perspective, using community, family, and individually-based techniques" (485). The project incorporated a family physician, a Navajo-speaking prevention worker and a Navajo-speaking clerk as part of the Community Health Services staff (485). This program was seen as successful by both participants in the study and community members who credited the staff members for "bridging the gap between the dominant culture and the Navajo culture" (489).

BEST PRACTICES IN SAFE AND HEALTHY
PREGNANCY CAMPAIGNS

The following discussion focuses on best practices in safe and healthy pregnancy initiatives and campaigns among AI/AN groups. These campaigns represent the shift we have witnessed in health campaigns overall that focus on community-level intervention versus the personal responsibility model. Community-based campaigns are locally driven and supported programs that may, and often do, use researchers, practitioners, and campaign materials both from within and outside the community to change attitudes, beliefs, and practices pertaining to an issue considered a risk. Some of the more recent successful community-based health campaigns have addressed topics including tobacco use, sustainable seafood choices, drinking and driving, and condom use (Lee and Kotler). The examples below, from between 1991 and 2012, illustrate the best practices of integrating cultural nuances, identity, and spirituality in community-based healthy pregnancy campaigns that include the voices of the AI/AN populations.

The Healthy Start Program

The Healthy Start Program, implemented in 1992, was one of only a handful of campaigns in the 1990s that included AI/AN. The program addressed infant mortality in targeted areas with high infant mortality rates and put pregnant women and new mothers in contact with health professionals and resources to help nurture the children (Howell et al. 25). The Northern Plains, which spans four states where nineteen American Indian tribal communities are located, was one of the selected areas for the program. Called the Northern Plains Healthy Start (NPHS), the program lasted from September 1991 to October 1997 (Howell et al. xiii). The program supported clients to assess the short- and long-term goals of their pregnancies with the ultimate aim of healthy pregnancies and babies (Giffin et al. 26). In line with these outcomes, the program supported women to keep smoke-free homes by placing culturally appropriate smoke-free signs and messages on doors and in areas of the home to remind people to smoke outside (BlueEye et al. 20).

Development of educational and promotional materials for the NPHS was guided by respect for the culture and values of American Indian families, including respect for Elders. Thus, community Elders and members were involved in all aspects of the program acting as role models. The program's emphasis on cultural values was seen as one of the factors that appealed to clients, and involving community members in developing the program helped the program gain legitimacy among the targeted audience as they took responsibility for it (Giffin et al. 26; Howell et al. 82). Evaluation of the program showed that it helped reduce adolescent birth rate, infant mortality, and increased general community knowledge and attitudes (Giffin et al. 27; Howell et al. 83).

American Indian Youth Challenge Program

The California Rural Indian Health Board was one of the earliest groups to provide teen pregnancy programming and has been providing community-based programming since 1996. The program is implemented in three sites in California and provides monthly comprehensive sexual health education session with a culturally appropriate approach, including traditional American Indian talking circles (Suellentrop and Hunter 5). Topics include birth control options, STI and HIV prevention, and delaying tactics. Although no formal evaluation has taken place, annual program improvement assessments do take place to determine if the program is meeting the needs of both the participants and the community (Suellentrop and Hunter 5).

The Yuonihan Project

The Yuonihan Project was developed by the Northern Plains American Indians in 2005 to prevent fetal alcohol spectrum disorders (FASDs). "Yuonihan" means "respect" or "to honour" in the Lakota language. It was a five-year Centers for Disease Control and Prevention (CDC) funded campaign to address FASD among Northern Plains American Indians. The aim of the campaign was to help Northern Plains American Indians communities understand FASD, address prevention, and to increase education and awareness (Hanson et al. 843). The campaign was developed with input from focus group discussions involving female tribal Elders, women of childbearing age, and other members of the community. Using this input, culturally relevant school and community-based pregnancy programs for American Indian youth were developed, which included family members and Elders in discussion, and culturally based activities and programs (844). Campaign materials included posters, radio ads, brochures, and pens featuring traditional Northern Plains American Indians symbols, including image of a turtle amulet and granddaughter dolls (844). The campaign materials were disseminated at strategic locations in the community. A survey assessment of the campaign indicted that it had increased knowledge about FASD among the target population and led to decrease in drinking patterns. The target population also rated the campaign as culturally appropriate (846).

Live It!

Live It! was a teen pregnancy prevention and sexual health program targeted at American Indian teens. The program was implemented between 2006 and 2008 with approximately seven hundred youth and ninety adults in more than sixty sites (Suellentrop and Hunter 5). This culturally specific program took a holistic approach to the wellbeing of youth, and emphasized the importance of integrating traditional values and teachings into teens' lives (Minnesota Department of Health). Developed by the Division of Indian Work in Minneapolis, with support from the Minnesota Department of Health, Eliminating Health Disparities Initiative, the Live It! program delivered a curriculum targeted at teens and another targeted at parents, guardians, and other adults working with teens (Suellentrop and Hunter 4). The curriculum addressed such issues as puberty, health relationships, and communication skills. Pre- and post-test evaluations of the program over the years showed it helped increase knowledge about sexual health issues among target audience (Suellentrop and Hunter 5). Program developers later worked to strengthen the pregnancy and sexually transmitted infection components, and to evaluate the impact on teens' behaviour.

The Coming of the Blessing

Created by the March of Dimes in 2007, this program provided prenatal educational curriculum using the American Indian symbol of the medicine wheel to describe the pregnancy cycle and infant care (Arnold et al.). What makes this program unique is that American Indian women from ten Nations conducted focus groups with providers and patients to develop the educational materials. Pilot project evaluation has shown promising results. For example, the preterm birth rate for AI/AN was 14.6 percent, but for women participating in the program, the rate dropped to 7 percent (Arnold et al. 5).

Cessation of Tobacco Use among Pregnant Women

This was a community participatory research intervention that began in 2007 aimed at addressing the problem of tobacco use among Alaska Native women residing in the Yukon Kuskokwim Delta. Research has shown that some 79 percent of Alaska Native women use tobacco during pregnancy (Patten 1); thus, the program aimed to address the issue. The intervention was a collaboration among the Yukon-Kuskokwim Health Corporation (YKHC), the Alaska Native Tribal Health Consortium (ANTHC) Board, and the Mayo Clinic Cancer Center, and it was part of a long-term plan to address health and welfare needs of children in the Yukon Kuskokwim Delta community. In developing the intervention program, individual interviews and focus group discussions were held with pregnant women and family members to gain an understanding of the components to be included in the program. Materials in the intervention program included counselling offered by an Alaska Native counsellor; pregnancy and culturally specific self-help materials; and videos of personal stories of pregnant women and other members of the community (Patten 88; Patten et al. 81). Women featured in the campaign videos modelled self-efficacy and desirable outcomes of quitting smoking. The evaluation of the program found that the intervention was highly acceptable and that retention of participants in the program was good. However, there was no evidence of the program leading to abstinence of use of tobacco products among pregnant women. This ineffectiveness could be due to the inappropriate approach program developers used to recruit participants. Participants were recruited over an eight-month period, and counselling was offered during prenatal hospital visits; follow-ups were done during late stages of the pregnancies (Patten 88; Patten et al. 83). However, some successful aspects of the program was that it was theory driven (i.e., social cognitive theory was the guiding theoretical framework). Moreover, it was designed in conjunction with members of the community who suggested appropriate means of disseminating campaign material and information, including use of personal stories.

Tips Campaign

The Tips from Former Smokers (Tips) Campaign is a paid, national tobacco education campaign developed by the CDC and launched in 2012. The campaign features real people living with the effects of smoking and second-hand smoking and health professionals who encourage smokers to quit smoking. The campaign is targeted at smokers between ages eighteen through fifty-four, focusing on parents, adolescents, healthcare providers, and faith communities (CDC). The campaign identified target groups including AI/AN and featured the stories of real people affected by smoking or second-hand smoking. Thus, the campaign aimed to address the urgency for smokers including pregnant women to quit smoking. An assessment of the Tips Campaign noted that it was effective in increasing attempts to quit smoking in the target population. A report on the campaign showed that 1.64 million smokers made an attempt to quit smoking after viewing the campaign; an estimated 4.7 million non-smokers recommended smoking cessation services to smokers; and 6 million people talked to smokers about the dangers of smoking after seeing the campaign (McAfee et al.).

SUMMARY

The campaigns described above demonstrate the importance of including the voices of target audiences in health campaigns in this case AI/AN populations. Recognizing the culture-specific challenges AI/AN face legitimizes their struggles and illustrates how campaigns must show respect for culture and heritage. This awareness can enhance mutual trust and lead to improvement in the health status of this group of people, becoming a win-win situation in which aims of the campaign are achieved and a community of people feels valued.

Yet in a study of thirty-one national health campaigns conducted among AI/AN groups by the Urban Health Institute in 2011, only two campaigns were aimed at safe and healthy pregnancies ("Looking to the Past" 27, 29). This could partially explain why the pregnancy rate among AI/ AN girls is alarmingly high compared to non-Hispanic whites (thirty-one births per one thousand compared to ten births per thousand) (Wiltz 3). These figures point to the lack of attention to this problem and the need for culturally appropriate campaigns. In this chapter, we recognize the role of culture, identity, and spirituality in successful AI/AN safe and healthy pregnancy campaigns and advocate for community-based campaigns as the basis for attitude and behaviuoral changes. We further advocate that the best practices include the voices of the AI/AN populations.

At the same time, we recognize the limitations of this work, primarily the lack of evaluative techniques of AI/AN safe and healthy pregnancy campaigns. In the 2011 Urban Indian Health Institute report, sixteen of the thirty-one campaigns lacked evaluative techniques (17). This indicates that campaign proposals must include funding for effective evaluation. In addition to funding, campaigns should also include culturally centred evaluative techniques—an emerging critical approach for studying health and culture (Dutta 304). Evelyn Ho emphasizes that a critical approach is necessary "to ensure that all voices are heard and that our work does not further oppress marginalized groups" (233). For example, evaluative tools could range from surveys designed to recognize the nuances among Nations to focus groups addressing the relationship of a Nation's spirituality to overall campaign effectiveness. Whether quantitative or qualitative evaluative techniques are used, the voices of those marginalized groups must be included in the development of these measurements.

The foci of this study are the issues related to the effects of colonialism on childbirth, pregnancy, babies, and mothers beginning with European contact in the fifteenth and sixteenth centuries that continue to affect Indigenous people. The well-known individual, national, and environmental damage inflicted upon Indigenous groups in North America—among those we call American Indians, Native Americans, Native Alaskans, and by the names of the 567 individual Nations—must not be dismissed as past history but should be regarded as a serious problem for Native people—especially babies and mothers. American Indians are neither disappearing, invisible, nor of little consequence.

Our focus on the need for sensitivity to cultural nuances, identity, and spirituality in safe and healthy pregnancy campaigns among AI/AN emerges from our passion for the ethical and equitable treatment of women and, as mothers, our passion for the sacred act of bringing new life into the world and for creating a better world for our own and our sisters' children. We desire a world where destructive behaviours of all sorts—all disempowering acts of those in power who situate American Indians on the margins—will not cause harm. We desire a world where there is no abuse of addictive substances, an abuse that disempowers our Nations, ourselves, and, most tragically, our children. The abuses arise from poverty, cultural deprivation, poor nutrition, and continued discrimination, all of which have arisen from colonialism—the origin of identity loss.

WORKS CITED

Alexander, Greg R., et al. "Pregnancy Outcomes of American Indians: Contrasts among Regions and With Other Ethnic Groups." *Maternal Child Health Journal* vol.12, suppl. 1, 2008, pp. 5-11.

Arnold, Carol M., et al. "The Coming of the Blessing: A Successful Cross-Cultural Col labourative Effort of American Indian/Alaska Native Families." *Family Community Health*, vol. 34, no. 3, 2011, pp. 196-201.

BlueEye, LaDonna, et al. "Native American Action Plan: Addressing Tobacco Abuse among Pregnant and Postpartum Women." *The National Partnership to Help Pregnant Smokers Quit,* June 2008, www.tobaccocessation.org/PDFs/NativeAmericanActionPlan. pdf. Accessed 25 Aug. 2017.

Brown, Leslie, et al. "Feminism and First Nations: Conflict or Concert?" *Canadian Review of Social Policy / Revue Canadiennme de Politique Sociale*, vol. 35, 1995, pp.68-78.

Centers for Disease Control and Prevention (CDC). *Tips from Former Smokers: Campaign Overview*, 11 Oct., 2016, www. cdc.gov/tobacco/campaign/tips/. Accessed 25 Aug. 2017.

Clawson, Roger. "The Alarming Increase in Alcohol-Damaged Children." *The Alicia Patterson Foundation*, 12 Apr. 12, 2011, www.aliciapatterson.org/stories/alarming-increase-alcohol-damaged-children. Accessed 25 Aug. 2017.

Curtin, Patricia A., and Kenn T. Gaither. "Ethical Considerations in Global Practice." *International Public Relations. Negotiating*

Culture, Identity, and Power, edited by Patricia A. Curtin et al., Sage, 2007, pp. 235-252.

Curtin, Patricia A., and Kenn T. Gaither. "Privileging Identity, Difference, and Power: The Circuit of Culture as a Basis for Public Relations Practice." *Journal of Public Relations Research,* vol. 17, no. 2, 2005, pp. 91-115.

Curtin, Patricia A., and Kenn T. Gaither. "Contested Notions of Identity in International Public Relations: The World Health Organization's Smallpox Eradication Campaign." *International Communication Association,* May 2005., New York, NY. Unpublished conference paper.

Dillard, Dana, and Jorene Olrun-Volkheimer. "Providing Culturally Sensitive Care for Pregnant Alaska Native Women and Families." *International Journal of Childbirth Education,* vol. 29, no. 1, 2014, pp. 62-7.

Dixon, Lynda. "Interactions between American Indian Women and Their White Male Doctor: The Stages of a Health Care Visit at a Public Health Facility." *Intercultural Communication Studies,* vol. 12, no. 1, 2003, pp. 43-58.

Dixon, Lynda. "The Cherokee Way: A Rhetorical Analysis of Principal Chief Chadwick A. 'Corntassel' Smith's Speech 'Let Us Build One Fire.'" *The Rhetoric of Western Thought,* 8th ed., edited by James Golden et al., Kendell/Hunt, 2004, pp. 429-38.

Dixon, Lynda, and Paul Shaver. "The Cultural Perspective of a Public Health Facility for Oklahoma American Indians: Architectural Changes as Organizational Rhetoric." *Rhetoric in Intercultural Contexts: International and Intercultural Communication Annual NCA, 22,* edited by Alberto Gonzalez and Delores Tanno, Sage, 2000, pp. 131-45.

Dutta, Mohan J. "Communicating About Culture and Health: Theorizing Culture-Centered and Cultural Sensitivity Approaches." *Communication Theory* vol. 17, no.3. 2007, pp. 304-28.

Flora, June A., et al. "Communication Campaigns to PreventCardiovascular Disease: The Stanford Community Studies." *Public Communication Campaigns,* 2nd ed., edited by Ronald E. Rice and Charles K. Atkin, Sage, 1989, pp. 233-52.

Garwick, Ann W., et al. "Native Teen Voices: Adolescent Pregnancy Prevention Recommendations." *Journal of Adolescent Health,* vol. 42, no. 1, 2008, pp. 81-8.

Giffin, Mary F., et al. "Telling the Healthy Start Story: A Report on the Impact of the 22 Demonstration Projects." *Arlington: National Center for Education in Maternal and Child Health*, 1999, www.nationalhealthystart.org/healthy_start_initiative. Accessed 25 Aug. 2017.

Goesling, Brian, et al. "Programs to Reduce Teen Pregnancy, Sexually Transmitted Infections, and Associated Sexual Risk Behaviors: A Systematic Review." *Journal of Adolescent Health*, vol. 54, no. 5, 2014, pp. 499-507.

Guttman, Nurit, and Charles T. Salmon. "Guilt, Fear, Stigma and Knowledge Gaps: Ethical Issues in Public Health Communication Interventions." *Bioethics*, vol. 18, no. 6, 2004, pp. 531-52.

Habermas, Jurgen. *The Theory of Communicative Action: Reason and the Rationalization of Society*. Vol 1. Polity, 2015.

Hall, Stuart. "Culture, Community, Nation." *Cultural Studies*, vol. 7, no. 3, 1993, pp. 349-63.

Hanson, Jessica D. "Understanding Prenatal Health Care for American Indian Women in a Northern Plains Tribe." *Journal of Transcultural Nursing*, vol. 23, no. 1, 2012, pp. 29-37.

Hanson, Jessica D., et al. "Development of a Media Campaign on Fetal Alcohol Spectrum Disorders for Northern Plains American Indian Communities." *Health Promotion Practice*, vol. 13, no. 6, 2012, pp. 842-847.

Hanson, Gaye. "A Relational Approach to Cultural Competence." *Restoring the Balance: First Nations Women, Community and Culture*, edited by Gail Guthrie Valaskakis et al., University of Manitoba Press, 2009, pp. 237-64.

Ho, Evelyn Y. "Socio-cultural Factors in Health Communication." *Health Communication: Theory, Method, and Application*, edited by Nancy Grant Harington, Routledge, 2015, pp. 212-39.

Hodge, Felicia, and Karabi Nandy. "Predictors of Wellness and American Indians." *Journal of Healthcare for the Poor and Underserved*, vol. 22, no. 3, 2011, pp. 791-803.

Holmes, Malcolm D., and Judith A. Antell. "The Social Construction of American Indian Drinking: Perceptions of American Indian and White Officials." *Sociological Quarterly*, vol. 42, no. 2, 2001, pp. 151-73.

Hornik, Robert. "Public Health Education and Communication as Policy Instruments for Bringing About Changes in Behavior." *Social Marketing: Theoretical and Practical Perspectives*, edited by Marvin E. Goldberg, et al., Lawrence Erlbaum Associates, 1997, pp. 45-58.

Howell, Embry M., et al. *Infant Mortality Prevention in American Indian Communities: Northern Plains Healthy Start*, 1 Jan., www.ideas.repec.org/p/mpr/mprres/f1dea9e-302304be287809858a3dfd2b3.html#cites. Accessed 25 Aug. 25 2017.

Indian Health Service. *HIS Joins Tobacco Cessation Campaign. Centers for Disease Control and Prevention*, 2013. www.ihs.gov/newsroom/index.cfm/announcements/2013announcements/ihsjoinstobaccocessationcampaign/. Accessed 25 Aug. 2017.

Kellner, Douglas. "Critical Theory and British Cultural Studies: The Missed Articulation." *Cultural Methodologies*, edited by Jim McGuigan, Sage, 1997, pp. 12-41.

Lee, Nancy R., and Philip Kotler. *Social Marketing: Influencing Behaviors for Good*. 4th ed. Sage, 2011.

Claudia R., and Mary Ann Curry. "Living in Two Worlds: Native American Women and Prenatal Care." *Health Care for Women International*, vol. 19, no. 3, 1998, pp. 205-15.

"Looking to the Past to Improve the Future: Designing a Campaign to Address Infant Mortality Among AI/AN." *Urban Indian Health Institute, Seattle Indian Health Board,* January, 2011, www.uihi.org/wp-content/uploads/2011/07/Healthy-Babies-Lit-Review-Final_JulyRev.pdf. Accessed 25 Aug. 2017.

Masis, Kathleen, and Philip May. "A Comprehensive Local Program for the Prevention of Fetal Alcohol Syndrome." *Public Health Reports*, vol.106, no. 5, 1991, pp. 484-89.

McAfee, Tim, et al. "Effect of the First Federally Funded U.S. Antismoking National Media Campaign." *Lancet*, vol. 382, no. 9909, 2013, pp. 2003-11.

Middlestadt, Susan E., et al. "Community Involvement in Health Planning: Lessons Learned From Practicing Social Marketing in a Context of Community Control, Participation, and Ownership." *Social Marketing: Theoretical and Practical Perspectives*, edited by Marvin Goldberg, et al., Lawrence Erlbaum

Associates, 1997, pp. 291-311.

Minnesota Department of Health. *Minnesota Evidence-Based PREP Curricula*, www.health.state.mn.us/divs/cfh/program/prep/curricula.cfm. Accessed 25 Aug. 2017.

National Institute on Alcohol Abuse and Alcoholism. *Alcohol Alert,* no. 13, PH 297, July 1991. www.pubs.niaaa.nih.gov/publications/aa13.htm. Accessed 25 Aug. 2017.

Neufeld, Hannah Tait. "Patient and Caregiver Perspectives of Health Provision Practices for First Nations and Métis Women With Gestational Diabetes Mellitus Accessing Care in Winnipeg, Manitoba." *BMC Health Services Research,* vol. 14, no. 1, 2014, pp. 1.

Patten, Christi A. "Tobacco Cessation Intervention during Pregnancy among Alaska Native Women." *Journal of Cancer Education,* vol. 27, no. 1, 2012, pp. S86-S90.

Patten, Christi A., et al. "Feasibility of a Tobacco Cessation Intervention for Pregnant Alaska Native Women." *Nicotine & Tobacco Research,* vol. 12, no. 2, 2010, pp. 79-87.

Perry, Cheryl L., and Steven Kelder. "Models for Effective Prevention." *Journal of Adolescent Health,* vol. 13, no. 5, 1992, pp. 355-63.

Rankin, James G. "From Scrubland to Vintage Wine: Australia's Response to Substance- Related Problems in the Last 40 Years." *Drug and Alcohol Review,* vol. 22, no. 3, 2003, pp. 255-62.

Rentner, Terry L., and Lara Lengel. "Ethical Dilemmas in Social Marketing Campaigns: A study of National and International Alcohol-Reduction Campaigns and Their Attention to Cultural Communities." *Ethics in International Communication,* edited by Alexander Nikolaev, Palgrave, 2011, pp. 137-53.

Rentner, Terry L., et al. "Critiquing Fetal Alcohol Syndrome Health Communication Campaigns Targeted to American Indians." *Journal of Health Communication,* vol. 17, no. 1, 2012, pp. 6-21.

Salmon, Charles T. "Campaigns for Social "Improvement: An Overview of Values, Rationales, and Impacts." *Information Campaigns: Balancing Social Values and Social Change,* edited by Charles Salmon, Sage, 1989, pp. 19-53.

Stone, Rosaline, et al. "Traditional Practices, Traditional Spirituality, and Alcohol Cessation among American Indians." *Journal of Studies on Alcohol,* vol. 67, no. 2, 2006, pp. 236-44.

Suellentrop, Katherine, and Grace Hunter. "Science Says #39: American Indian/ Alaska Native Youth and Teen Pregnancy Prevention." *The National Campaign to Prevent Teen and Unplanned Pregnancy,* Aug. 2009, www.thenationalcampaign.org/resource/science-says-39. Accessed 25 Aug. 2017.

Turpel, Mary Ellen. "Patriarchy and Paternalism: The Legacy of the Canadian State for First Nations Women." *Canadian Journal of Women and the Law,* vol. 6, no.1, 1993, pp. 174-192.

Whitbeck, Les, et al. "Discrimination, Historical Loss and Enculturation: Culturally Specific Risk and Resiliency Factors for Alcohol Abuse among American Indians." *Journal of Studies on Alcohol,* vol. 65, no. 4, 2004, pp. 409-18.

Wiltz, Teresa. "Racial and Ethnic Disparities Persist in Teen Pregnancy Rates." *The Pew Charitable Trusts,* 3 Mar. 2015, www.pewtrusts.org/en/research-and-analysis/blogs/stateline/2015/3/03/racial-and-ethnic-disparities-persist-in-teen-pregnancy-rates. 25 Aug. 2017.

Winkleby, Marilyn A., et al. "The Influence of Gender and Socioeconomic Factors on Hispanic/White Differences in Body Mass Index." *Preventive Medicine* vol. 25, no.2, 1996, pp 203-11.

II. Birth

4.

Bored, Broke, and Alone

Experiences of Pregnant and Expectant First Nations Mothers Birthing in and out of the Community

JAIME CIDRO, ELISABETH DOLIN, AND CHRISTINA QUESKEKAPOW

A DEATH IN A First Nations community is a collective event. Offices and stores shut down, and funeral celebrations last for several days as the community rallies to support the families. On the other hand, the birth of a baby is often entirely removed from the community as women are forced to travel long distances, often alone, to deliver their baby. In Norway House Cree Nation, returning the practice of birthing in the community has been a much debated and discussed topic in the community, especially given that Norway House has a hospital with physicians as well as midwifery services. Over more than a decade, funders, policy-makers, practitioners, and the community have met the call for the return of birthing with various responses, but access to local birth services remains elusive. In 2012 a research project, in partnership with the community and a research team, began to explore the issues around returning birthing to the community. This chapter describes the research process and some of the views and experiences of women giving birth both in the community and outside of the community. Specifically, the chapter focuses on women's isolation and the financial burden of having babies.

BACKGROUND

Canada's maternity care services are in decline in rural and remote communities because of a shortage of maternity care providers (family physicians, obstetricians, nurses, and midwives) and the centralization of services (Society of Obstetricians and Gynaecologists of Canada, *SOGC Policy Statement* 1186; Kornelsen and Gryzbowski 329). With few practitioners prepared to set up practice in rural or northern settings, giving birth close to home has become a significant concern across the country; the medical literature and public media often discuss it. Traditionally, Canadian women, particularly First Nations women, gave birth in their home communities, among friends and relatives. Cultural practices established strong community roots for the mother, her infant, the family. The children born in the community developed a clear sense of identity helping them to become resilient and responsible members of that community. Ceremonies to welcome babies into the world and to support the family were common occurrences. Kim Anderson describes the arrival of a baby and the role of the community: "Birth! The old mosoms and the old kohkoms were all there. They were always available. They were those holy men and women who blessed you with their praise, when they came and saw a new child.' Depending on the circumstances and who was available at the time, the birth of a baby involved various members of the community" (46).

Midwives have long played an integral role in First Nations communities. Anderson describes the role of midwives assisting not only with births in First Nations communities and settlements but also with the newly forming settler communities. One of her participants describes midwifery in northern Saskatchewan: "Indian babies, Métis babies and French babies...Even our school teacher—whenever his wife had a baby he used to come and get my grandmother and she used to go stay there and wait for the baby" (48).

Decline and resurgence often characterizes the history of midwifery. Rachel Olson describes the connections between the medicalization of birthing and the uneven application of midwifery practices as depending on a number of factors across Canada including geography and location, politics and the economy (34). Margaret McDonald describes the shift to hospital birthing in the 1940s, resulting in the decline of the midwife (237). Across Canada, an uneven distribution of policies to limit the midwives' ability to practice has resulted in a varied history from province to province. The history of the midwifery profession can be summarized as follows: "Traditional, women-centered, home-based midwifery birth culture of the 19th century was stamped out at the hands of the rising medical profession and the march of progress. A new kind of midwifery later emerged in the 1970s as a grassroots social movement, eventually achieving full legal and professional recognition in the 1990s" (McDonald 237).

The midwifery profession that gained traction in the 1970s and became professionalized in the 1990s was based on the restoration of "birth as a natural event; to reinvent women as competent birthers and attendants; and to restore the location of birth to the home"; this was largely due to the inaccessibility of hospitals for birthing (McDonald 237). By the late 1980s, midwives became part of the informal health care system in Ontario; they focused on giving more control to birthing women (McDonald 239). In the years that followed, midwifery education and formalized colleges developed across Canada, and the profession became recognized.

While midwifery as a profession became reestablished across Canada, women in rural and remote communities began to give birth more frequently in hospitals to decrease maternal mortality and morbidity. For First Nations women, in particular, this meant being transferred out of their home community weeks before their due date (called confinement), which often resulted in many negative social consequences, including a disconnection from the community (Society of Obstetricians and Gynaecologists of Canada, *SOGC Policy Statement* 1187; Chamberlain and Barclay 117). Although midwives are well established across most urban and some rural and northern communities, the maternal medical relocation model (sometimes referred to as "evacuation for birth" or "birthing evacuation policy"), requiring women be "sent out for confinement", remains the dominant approach toward First Nations women in remote reserve communities.

Policymakers in Canada have begun to question this practice and have acknowledged its negative impact on women, their families, and their communities. The resurgence of interest in midwifery services across Canadian Indigenous communities has become more prevalent. Still, often unaccompanied, women must leave their communities to experience labour and delivery in a distant referral centre where they reside in short-term boarding houses for weeks, which leaves them feeling culturally alienated or isolated over the course of the birthing period. Teenage girls may be particularly vulnerable when left without their mothers or caregivers for weeks at a critical time in their development (Chamberlain and Barclay 117).

In an interview for the *Ottawa Citizen*, fifty-three-year-old Tulugak, an Inuk from Nunavut, describes that he, like many of his generation, was born in an igloo. Each of his five children, however, was born in Moose Factory. "My kids were born to strangers," he says. "I felt a bit angry about not being there." He also believes that dislocation among fathers and family members contributed to "social and cultural upheaval" as well as domestic violence, substance abuse, and, in some cases, suicide (qtd. in Payne). He likens the relocation of birth to that of evacuating children out of their communities to attend residential school. Stories like this can be found across Canadian Indigenous communities. The small First Nations community Bella Bella, located on Waglisla Island on the central coast of British Columbia, has a long history of providing local intrapartum care. With a full-service hospital and operative capability, it successfully provided maternity services for eighty years. In 2000, with unreliable Caesarean section capability, the service closed. As with many parturient women across Canada, Bella Bella women now deliver in distant centres (Iglesias et al. e235). As part of a larger case study investigating the variables causing the demise of Bella Bella's obstetric services, Kornelsen et al. have documented women's experiences of birth locally and away. The interviews with women who gave birth at home provide a story of belonging, which reflect qualities of culture and identity, wellbeing, and the interconnectedness of life and death ("Geography of Belonging" 642). The establishment of birthing centres in Nunavik, for example, directly connects to larger constructs of community healing. Vickie Wagner and her colleagues describe community birthing as an essential component of restoring skills and pride and in capacity building in the community. Moreover, they stress its importance as a mechanism for building family and community relationships and intergenerational support and learning through promoting traditional knowledge and teaching transcultural skills (390).

BIRTHING AWAY AND STRESS

The experience of birthing carries its own set of stress, but within a rural and remote context, with few maternity services, this stress is exacerbated. Parturient women who had to travel more than one hour to access services were 7.4 times more likely to experience moderate or severe stress when compared to women who had local access to maternity services. This stress is amplified for parturient women with children remaining at home (Kornelsen et al., "Stress and Anxiety" 11). These experiences of stress also extend to financial anxiety. The financial costs of extended stays away from home—such as travel, accommodation, and food expenses—can become burdensome for many women and families (13). In remote Manitoban First Nations communities, travel and accommodation costs are covered only for the expectant mother. Unless the woman is deemed to be in need of medical support or in need of services such as translation, any escorts that may choose to accompany her on her journey will shoulder the costs themselves (First Nations and Inuit Health). The "escort policy" has recently changed to allow for a funded escort paid for by FNIH. There is also significant relationship between socioeconomic status and prenatal care, as the majority of First Nations families on reserves live in poverty (Heaman et al., "Prevalence" 243). The Manitoba Regional Health Survey (2008-2010), which looks at First Nations people living on reserves in Manitoba, reports that almost 25.7 percent of families have a total personal income of less than $10,000 per year, and 51.8 percent report household incomes below $30,000 per year (Assembly of Manitoba Chiefs). In comparison, the median income in 2010 for the non-Aboriginal population in Canada was $27,600, and for First Nations specifically it was $17,600 (Statistics Canada "Aboriginal Peoples").

First Nations communities incur great costs supporting women evacuated to give birth; recent research has found that the average cost for giving birth in a referral centre to be $3,732.87 (Kornelsen et al. "Alienation"). In Kornelsen's research of thirty-one evacuated women from British Columbia, the total amount incurred by the band council was $115,719 to support travel, accommodation, and sustenance (59). Psychosocial stress of giving birth is also exacer-

JAIME CIDRO, ELISABETH DOLIN, AND CHRISTINA QUESKEKAPOW

bated when maternal care is no longer provided in communities. Other research suggests psychosocial consequences of evacuation. Once a community event, birth becomes an isolating experience; women no longer control their birthing experience (Kornelsen et al., "Geography of Belonging" 644). Marie Chamberlain and Kate Barclay have highlighted three main stressors to women evacuated for birth: (1) emotional stress from forced separation from family, culture, and community; (2) physical stress relating to challenges in finding adequate assistance; and (3) economic stressors for childcare for current children as well as financial burdens to bring along partners or other supports (118). The effect of stress on unborn babies is not well understood in the literature, although overall stress has been associated with preterm birth (Ruiz et al. 55).

RETURNING BIRTHING TO NORWAY HOUSE CREE NATION

Norway House Cree Nation (NHCN) has a strong interest in returning birthing services to the community. NHCN is one of the largest First Nations communities in Manitoba. It is located where the Nelson River and Lake Winnipeg meet, about 456 kilometers north of Winnipeg and an eight-hour drive. Norway House had a population of 4,758 in 2011. With a population of 4,071 in 2006, the community had grown by 16.9 percent in only five years (Statistics Canada, "Census"). According to NHCN band membership office, the 2015 population was 6,918 people, with 162 babies born in that year, which represents a crude birth rate of 23.4 percent. NHCN also shares its territory with the "town site" of Norway House, which is not reserve land and is governed by a mayor and council. A large non-status and Métis population lives in this part of the community. The establishment of a birthing centre—such as those in Nunavik, Québec—has been on the radar for NHCN for many years. As with many rural Canadians communities, the women of Norway House cannot deliver their babies in their home community and are usually evacuated to Thompson or Winnipeg. The current Norway House Indian Hospital, one of two remaining federally run hospitals in the country, was originally built in 1952 as a sixteen-bed, four-bassinet facility. Until the 1970s, women in NHCN could give birth at the community hospital unless they were assessed as a high-risk pregnancy or potentially high-risk delivery, at which time they were evacuated to a tertiary centre such as Winnipeg or Thompson for care.

Since 2006, there have been government-funded midwifery services in Norway House. In recent years, the provincially funded Kinosao Sipi Midwifery Clinic (KSMC), operating as part of the clinic within the hospital, has provided primary pre-natal, postnatal, and newborn care, and has arranged referrals to urban hospitals for intrapartum care. Recently, the KSMC reduced services when the sole midwife had to leave the commu-nity for family reasons. The midwife now provides care in the community on a part-time fly-in basis working with other care providers such as the physicians, and works with the community to establish group prenatal care, and supports orientation and training of other primary-care providers in this emerging care model. Women still travel to give birth.

In Manitoba, a recent report, "Perinatal Services and Outcomes in Manitoba" provides a statistical snapshot of Manitoban women travelling to give birth (Heaman et al., *Perinatal* 152). Almost half of women (46.8 percent) in Manitoba travel outside their regional health authority to give birth. In terms of distance travelled, one quarter (25.2 percent) of women travel more than 113.8 kilometers, whereas half (50.6 percent) travel more than 46.7 kilometers (the median distance). The rate of travelling more than 113.8 kilome-ters was identified as highest in the regional health authorities of Interlake (29.7 percent), North Eastman (31.8 percent), Churchill (97.1 percent), and Northern (73.8 percent). NHCN women would be represented in the Northern Health Authority region. According to the report, women travelling more than 113.8 kilometers to give birth are likely to be younger, to live in lower-income families, to be lone parents, and to be multiparous (Heaman et al., *Perinatal* 158). In Manitoba, nearly one quarter of all births in First Nations communities are to teen mothers, of which 90 percent are to single mothers (Manitoba Health). Little information was available on individual First Nations communities such as Norway House for this study, which made it challenging for informed discussion and decision making about the possibility of returning birthing services to the community.

As a response to the need for community specific data, the "Repatriating Birthing" project was initiated, which explores the social, cultural, and clinical feasibility of birth repatriation in NHCN using a three pronged approach exploring: (a) attitudes of primary-care staff and the community; (b) the experiences of Norway House women who have left the community to birth as well as the experiences of women who have given birth in the community since before 1970, and (c) the clinical feasibility of supporting low-risk mothers and their neonates in the community and the subsequent costs of evacuation. The focus of this chapter is to describe some of the stresses associated with leaving the community to give birth for women in NHCN and will not include a discussion on attitudes of primary-care staff or a clinical feasibility. At the time of this publication, this data has not yet been published.

THE RESEARCH PROCESS

In 2012, the community initiated a research partnership to better understand the perspectives of the community and healthcare providers around returning birthing services to the community. Partners at the community level (NHCN Health Division and Midwifery Services) and the regional level (Northern Medical Unit, Assembly of Manitoba Chiefs) worked with University of Winnipeg researchers to design a research project that met the evidence needs of NHCN. The project began with the development of a Community Advisory Circle (CAC) consisting of Elders (male and female), clinic staff, hospital staff, maternal child health workers, and the local Chief and Council. The CAC worked with the research team to decide what questions would be asked, how they would be asked, and to provide support to recruit participants. Throughout the data collection process, CAC meetings presented initial findings and assisted in the analysis and community contextualization of the findings.

The CAC also provided oversight on knowledge dissemination and translation activities. Integral to the process was the adherence to OCAP (ownership, control, access, and possession) (Schnarch 80) principles as well as to the First Nations Ethical Research principles developed at the Assembly of Manitoba Chiefs. These principles allowed the development of a research agreement, which was bound through a band council resolution. The research agreement developed with the CAC focuses on (a) the structure and role of the CAC; (b) the support of Chief and Council in the project; (c) the storage of the data during data collection; (d) the storage of data with the First Nations Health and Social Secretariat of Manitoba post-project; and (e) the process in place to ensure community ownership of the data to maximize the usage. This was the first comprehensive research agreement developed in NHCN and is an example of how to effectively operationalize the OCAP and First Nations ethical research principles. This foundation was important to the spirit of the research project and resulted in a smooth process with full community support.

Semi-structured qualitative interviews were conducted with thirty-one women to identify deeper understandings of their experiences. There were a total of 127 birth experiences described by the thirty-one women interviewed. Of those births, fourteen took place in Norway House, twenty in Thompson, eighty-eight in Winnipeg, and five in another location. Of the local births, seven occurred recently, or after 2007 (when the midwifery clinic opened), and seven occurred before 2007. The research associate and the local community researcher conducted the interviews with the participants. Key questions, developed with the Community Advisory Circle, framed the interviews, and participants were encouraged to introduce additional topics they considered important. This flexible approach allowed for discovery or elaboration of important information that may not have been previously considered by the researchers. Preliminary findings presentations were conducted in the community with participants, the Community Advisory Circle, and the local Chief and Council. Once approved for knowledge translation outside of the community, preliminary findings were shared. Presenting information in the community assisted in further analysis of the findings and contributed to understanding some of the local context, which has affected maternity services, such as when the hospital had a full complement of physicians or other issues affecting services.

A paucity of research exists on this topic; thus, the principles of grounded theory methodology were used, in which the collected data becomes the foundation of the theory leading to the development of themes and concepts (Strauss and Corbin). Grounded theorists start with "data and construct these data through observations, interactions and materials gathered about the topic or setting" (Charmaz 3). This project took a relational approach, which is consistent with Indigenous research methodologies such as those described by Shawn Wilson. These provide an important methodological framework for understanding relationships between the researcher, participant, community, and topic (Wilson 10). Grounded theory and several Indigenous research methodologies have similar foundations because of their shared focus on the process of interrelationships (Wilson 10; Absolon 85).

Interviews were recorded, transcribed, and coded using NVIVO software. During the early process of coding, the researchers sorted, separated, and synthesized data. They then posed analytic questions to the participants and community partners, which allowed for fuller distillation of themes (Charmaz 113). After draft sets of themes were identified, the researchers returned to the community to share preliminary findings with stakeholders and research participants in a variety of formats. Emergent themes were concurred by stakeholders and participants, and additional analysis of the themes was provided. A range of themes emerged from the interviews, which included continuity of care, issues with travel, support at referral centres, breastfeeding support, and delayed family planning. This chapter focuses on the personal stress and anxiety of interview participants.

WHAT THE WOMEN SAID

Giving birth to a baby is an emotional journey. Birthing women require support and love while they are giving birth but also during the time leading up to the delivery and the time after delivery. The participants spent a great deal of time discussing the emotional aspects of giving birth. The most common theme emerging from women describing their experiences as expectant mothers was loneliness and isolation. Women described being without an escort and travelling alone to give birth in a city. They also described feeling anxiety and loneliness for their children who stayed in the community. One participant described the heartache around missing her family while she gave birth in Winnipeg:

> The main thing for me is family. It was hard to leave home. You're always home, and you really don't go anywhere. Leaving everyone and going on your own makes it harder. There's a lot of crying, and you just want to go home [crying]. Somebody should always have somebody with them to go have their babies. It is hard to be alone over there to go have your babies.

In some cases, especially for the younger women, they have little experience in an urban centre. Travelling without an escort can be particularly daunting, even while they are staying in the community boarding home. One participant described her experience:

> I never went anywhere on my own. This was the first time I left Norway House, was to go have a baby. I was nervous and scared. I had to stay in a boarding home, and I really didn't know anybody. My husband wasn't able to come with me, so I just stayed out there for two weeks in a boarding home. It was really lonely. I was scared to go out because I was scared I would get lost. I didn't know anyone. I would have anxiety thinking about going across the street to go get juice.

The loneliness felt by expectant mothers birthing alone can become exacerbated when they do not feel supported by their primary healthcare providers. Another participant described this isolation:

> Lonely. I was emotional most of the time while I was there by myself. I wish I had this one nurse that I had during the day. She was really good. She talked to me and told me what to expect. The night nurses didn't even come check on me. I was scared because it was my first baby, and I didn't even know how to push. They didn't teach me how to push or what to expect when the baby comes out. It was really awful to see this baby coming out like that.

The effects of having to leave the community can also result in financial strain. Participants described challenges around finding and paying for babysitting, phone calls, and cell phone bills. If they have family members who can come to the centre with them, the costs associated with their stay (food and accommodation) are not covered. One participant, who had her babies both in Norway House and Winnipeg, described the cost of the Winnipeg birth: "If I had to guess, I think it was probably around three thousand dollars. We ate out a lot, and it was the food that added the most. There was no kitchen there [at the boarding house]. That would have probably made a big difference." Another participant described concerns around her husband missing work to come to Thompson when she was ready to deliver: "I called him when I went into labour. I called him that morning, and I told him that I wasn't sure but he could come now. He wasn't sure either. He couldn't miss work. He had one more day of work to do. I went to the hospital and checked to see for sure, and they put me on a monitor, and I was contracting. So he came." Another participant discussed the connection between financial concerns and stress for the mother: "Mentally it isn't healthy. You have mothers stressing out in the city and worrying about their families back home, and worrying if needs are being met. And you're stretching your dollar. Instead of focusing on your finances for home, you have to stretch it for Winnipeg also. You still need to buy baby clothes and formula. That costs a lot."

Some of the single-parent participants described some of the stresses of leaving children at home without sufficient support. As one respondent discussed: "You've seen them, they're stressed out and a lot of them are single parents. It's hard for them to leave. A lot of them have families here, and they can't leave their other kids. Everybody else has his or her own families to take care of. It's hard to leave your family and it's hard to leave your kids." Remarkably, several participants discussed having to rely on Child and Family Services for support for the children who remained at home. One participant talked about how her friends had to use the agency: "There were parents that actually signed their kids back into care or signed their kids to the agency because they had no choice. They had to go to Winnipeg to have their babies, and there was nobody else to watch their kids. They have no other resources, so they surrender their kids to the agency temporarily."

Participants also described the travel services as being especially stressful. Women are typically transported by medical bus to give birth or, in some cases, by plane. Until recently, women came home with their newborn baby on the same medical bus, a ride lasting eight hours or more if they are coming back from Winnipeg. One participant described her experiences travelling from Winnipeg and the challenges of breastfeeding:

> I didn't like the long ride home. I had to keep my eyes closed most of the way. You have to breastfeed with people staring at you too. I felt so uncomfortable, and there were a lot of people around me. I didn't even have formula, so I had no choice but to feed him. I put a blanket over him. That was a very uncomfortable ride home. Those seats are so close together that my knees were right against the seat. I had a hard time feeding my son.

Throughout the duration of the project, an increasing number of women have made the decision to remain in the community to birth with the help of the midwife and physicians. This project interviewed a number of these women, and we can expect this trend to continue. In discussing her decision and considering others envisioning birthing in the community, one participant stated: "I think there were a lot of people that were making up their minds to stay here. I think that made us decide that we weren't going out for the last one. I think the mentality of a lot of people now, they just decide that they are not going out." Another participant who had her baby in NHCN described what a difference it made to the experience of stress: "It was a really good experience this last time. There was no stress. It wasn't stressful financially, and we didn't have to worry about babysitters and trying to buy stuff for the kids."

DISCUSSION

These findings represent a mere snapshot of the wealth of information provided by the participants on their experiences of loneliness, views on stress, risk and confinement, and service provision. Loneliness and boredom go hand in hand. Many of the women who birthed outside of NHCN, even those fortunate enough to have a spouse or escort, felt lonely. Although the confinement period is supposed to provide a time for a woman to gather her strength for the upcoming birth, the source of her strength—her family, spouse, and children—is often four to ten hours away. As mentioned above, women who are more than one hour away from home are far more likely to experience moderate or severe stress. Women used to being surrounded by family and friends, perhaps working or caring for existing children, are now forced to sit and wait alone for labour to begin.

FINANCIAL COSTS

The financial support provided for women has diminished over time, although only recently have there been announcements of increased support for escorts. The availability of First Nations and Inuit Health Branch (FNIHB) funded escorts is also very limited, so women and families are asked to increasingly take on more and more financial burden when they are sent away to give birth. For many women in NHCN, these financial costs cause a great deal of stress to the household and extended families. Additionally, women must also shoulder financial costs of providing childcare to her other children while she is away giving birth. In worst-case scenarios, women have been forced to surrender their children into the child and family services system, which has a whole range of negative implications. Although personal financial costs were not directly investigated in the research, several respondents reported spending almost four thousand dollars for sustenance, travel, accommodation and childcare for existing children, which corresponds, as shown above, to other research (Kornelsen et al., "Alienation"). The financial costs only add to the stress and anxiety felt by women and families (Chamberlain and Barclay 120).

Giving birth should be a joyous milestone. However for women in remote and northern communities, such as Norway House, the experience becomes a lonely one because they are forced to give birth alone in a strange city. It is also stressful for those women having to leave their other children with the community. The financial strains of travelling and living away from home for weeks can place undue hardship on families, many of which already suffer from poverty. All of this stress affects women as they prepare to give birth and after the baby is born. The future of maternity services is important for a community such as Norway House, which has a very young population. In 2011, Indigenous people in general represented the youngest demographic in the country with a median age of twenty-eight years, compared to the Canadian median age of forty-one years (Statistics Canada, "Aboriginal Statistics"). First Nations people in particular had a median age of twenty-six years, as 18.4 percent of the population was in the fifteen to twenty-five age bracket, compared to 12.0 percent of the Canadian population ("Aboriginal Statistics"). With this young population, the number of births will only continue to increase. The low life expectancy and high birth rates characterizing Aboriginal people in Canada result in a "young, quickly growing population" (Richmond and Cook 4). Between 2006 and 2011, First Nations people had an overall population increase of 22.9 percent. First Nations women are having babies younger than the general population; women under the age of twenty-five represented half of the women who had babies (Statistics Canada "Aboriginal Peoples"). This chapter provides only a glimpse into the depth of narrative experience provided by participants. Repatriating birthing continues to be at the forefront of health related concerns in this community and many other First Nations communities in Canada.

NEXT STEPS

In 2003, NHCN initiated the pursuit of managing, controlling, and administering its community health services, and became incorporated as the Norway House Health Services Incorporated under the Manitoba Corporations Act. The community spent several years developing a service plan and a health integration initiative. The need for maternal and newborn care—including a birthing centre incorporating the services of midwives and nurses to provide care before, during, and after birth for low-risk mothers—was identified as one of the gaps in programs the health integration initiative would address. The results of this research will assist the community and partners as they consider further options for service provision. This project has also provided an opportunity for the community to work with university researchers and other partners in a truly collaborative research model, which embraces OCAP principles and the mantra "no research about us, without us!" This project provides a basis for other communities interested in understanding their maternity care needs by looking at the issue from multiple perspectives: from the women having babies, from the care providers who work with pre- and postnatal mothers, and from the community welcoming new community members.

WORKS CITED

Absolon, Kathleen E. *Kaandosswin: How We Come to Know.* Fernwood Publishing, 2011.

Anderson, Kim. *Life Stages and Native Women: Memory, Teachings, and Story Medicine.* Vol. 15. University of Manitoba Press, 2011.

Assembly of Manitoba Chiefs (AMC). *First Nations Regional Health Survey (RHS).* Phase 2. Revised November 2012 edition. Assembly of Manitoba Chiefs, June 2012.

Chamberlain, Marie, and Kate Barclay. "Psychosocial Costs of Transferring Indigenous Women from their Community for Birth." *Midwifery*, vol. 16, no. 2, 2000, pp. 116-22.

Charmaz, Kathy. *Constructing Grounded Theory.* Sage, 2014.

First Nations and Inuit Health Branch. "Non-Insured Health Benefits Program Medical Transportation Policy Framework." *Health Canada*, 2005, www.hc-sc.gc.ca/fniah-spnia/alt_formats/fnihb-dgspni/pdf/pubs/medtransp/2005_med-transp-frame-cad-re-pdf. Accessed 26 Aug. 2017.

Heaman, Maureen et al. *Perinatal Services and Outcomes in Manitoba.* Manitoba Centre for Health Policy, 2012

Heaman, Maureen I., et al. "Prevalence and Predictors of Inadequate Prenatal Care: A Comparison of Aboriginal and Non-Aboriginal Women in Manitoba." *Journal of Obstetrics and Gynaecology Canada*, vol. 27, no. 3, 2005, pp. 237-48.

Iglesias, Aleandra, et al. "Birth in Bella Bella: Emergence and Demise of a Rural Family Medicine Birthing Service." *Canadian family physician Medecin de famille canadien*, vol. 56, no. 6, 2010, pp. 233-40.

Kornelsen, Jude, and Stefan Grzybowski. "Is Local Maternity Care an Optional Service in Rural Communities?" *Journal of Obstetrics and Gynecology Canada*, vol. 27, no. 4, 2005, pp. 329-31.

Kornelsen, Jude, et al. "Alienation and Resilience: The Dynamics of Birth Outside their Community for Rural First Nations Women." *International Journal of Indigenous Health*, vol. 7, no. 1, 2011, pp. 55-64.

Kornelsen, Jude, et al. "The Geography of Belonging: the Experience of Birthing at Home for First Nations Women." *Health & Place*, vol. 16, no. 4, 2010, pp. 638-45.

Kornelsen, Jude, et al. "Stress and Anxiety Associated with Lack of Access to Maternity Services for Rural Parturient Women." *Australian Journal of Rural Health*, vol. 19, no. 1, 2011, pp. 9-14.

Manitoba Health. *Chief Provincial Public Health Officer's Report on the Health Status of Manitobans 2010: Priorities for Prevention: Everyone, Every Place, Every Day.* Manitoba Health, 2011.

McDonald, Margaret. "Gender Expectations: Natural Bodies and Natural Births in the New Midwifery in Canada." *Medical Anthropology Quarterly*, vol. 20, no. 2, 2006, pp. 235-56.

Olson, Rachel. *Relocating Childbirth: the politics of birthplace and Aboriginal midwifery in Manitoba, Canada.* Dissertation. University of Sussex, 2013.

Payne, Elizabeth. "The Residential Schools of Medicine: Evacuating Women Out of Remote Communities to Give Birth is Traumatic, Harmful to Communities and Costly. So Why is it Still Happening?" *Ottawa Citizen*, 26 Nov. 2010.

Richmond, Chantel A.M., and Catherine Cook. "Creating Conditions for Canadian Aboriginal Health Equity: The Promise of Healthy Public Policy." *Public Health Reviews*, vol. 37, no. 2, 2016, pp. 1-16.

Ruiz, R.J., et al. "Predicting Risk of Preterm Birth: The Roles of Stress, Clinical Risk Factors, and Corticotropin-Releasing Hormone." *Biological research for nursing*, vol. 4, no. 1, 2002, pp. 54-64.

Schnarch, Brian. "Ownership, Control, Access, and Possession

(OCAP) Or Self-Determination Applied to Research: A Critical Analysis of Contemporary First Nations Research and some Options for First Nations Communities." *International Journal of Indigenous Health*, vol. 1, no. 1, 2004, pp. 80-95.

Society of Obstetricians and Gynaecologists of Canada. "SOGC Policy Statement. no. 251: Returning Birth to Aboriginal, Rural, and Remote Communities." *Journal of obstetrics and gynecology Canada: JOGC = Journal d'obstetrique et gynecologie du Canada: JOGC*, vol. 32, no.12, Dec. 2010, pp. 1186-88.

Statistics Canada. "Aboriginal Peoples in Canada: First Nations People, Metis and Inuit, National Household Survey, 2011." *Statistics Canada*, 2015, www12.statcan.gc.ca/nhs-enm/2011/as-sa/99-011-x/99-011-x2011001-eng.cfm. Accessed 20 June 2016.

Statistics Canada. "Aboriginal Statistics at a Glance." *Statistics Canada*, 2015. www.statcan.gc.ca/pub/89-645-x/89-645-x2010001-eng.htm. Accessed 26 Aug. 2017.

Statistics Canada. "Census of Population. Norway House 17, Manitoba (Indian reserve) 2011."

Statistics Canada, 2012, www12.statcan.gc.ca/mobile/2011/cp-pr/table-eng.cfm?SGC=4622058. Accessed 24 Nov. 2012.

Strauss, Anselm, and Juliet Corbin. "Grounded Theory Methodology." *Handbook of Qualitative Research*, vol. 17, edited by Norman Denzin and Yvonna Lincoln, 1994, pp. 273-85.

Wagner, Vicki, et al. "Reclaiming Birth, Health, and Community: Midwifery in the Inuit Villages of Nunavik, Canada." *Journal of Midwifery & Women's Health*, vol. 52, no. 4, 2007, pp. 384-91.

Wilson, Shawn. *Research Is Ceremony: Indigenous Research Methods*. Fernwood Publishing, 2008.

5.
Bearing Witness

Rural Indigenous Women's Experiences
of Childbirth in an Urban Hospital

RACHEL OLSON

MATERNAL EVACUATION is the practice of relocating pregnant women from rural and remote communities to deliver their baby in urban, tertiary hospitals. This common practice reflects the experience of most Indigenous women living in northern Canada today. The repatriation of birth back to Indigenous communities is central in most discussions of current Indigenous pregnancy and birth practices. The discourse of evacuation often centres on the presence or absence of a tertiary hospital facility; yet the hospital as a site of social interaction is rarely critically examined. In this chapter, Indigenous women's experiences of birth in the hospital setting are explored as a way of addressing this gap. The chapter is based on my PhD fieldwork and took place from September 2009 to December 2010. The study was a multisited ethnography that focused on the politics of birthplace for Indigenous women in Manitoba. After navigating various ethics processes,[1] I gained unprecedented access to the inner workings of a labour and delivery ward in a tertiary hospital in Manitoba, Canada. Because of this access, my role as a researcher shifted from one engaged in ethnographic fieldwork to one of *bearing witness* to the reality of current childbirth practices for Indigenous women. The chapter focuses on the stories of three, relocated Indigenous women, and I examine their birth stories to better understand how maternal evacuation is created, realized, and managed in the everyday practices of the hospital. By doing so, the hospital shifts from being a bounded space of highly order, biomedical regulation to a complex site of social interactions encompassing broader notions of health, social relations, and Indigenous nationhood.

BEARING WITNESS: POSITIONALITY

To better understand my role as a researcher in this setting, I must first locate myself within the research. I was born in Whitehorse, Yukon, with an Indigenous father and an Irish-French mother, and identify myself as a citizen of the Tr'ondek Hwech'in First Nation. I attempted to become a midwife in 2004, entering and quickly exiting a bachelor of midwifery programme at the University of British Columbia. After this attempt at becoming a midwife, I worked in the policy setting for the National Aboriginal Health Organization (NAHO), and then during my PhD as a consultant for multiple stakeholders, including the National Aboriginal Council of Midwives (NACM). I wrote various reports and policy documents, for the federal government, the provincial government of Manitoba, and Aboriginal organizations. I was firmly ensconced in the policy world of Aboriginal midwifery and an active advocate for midwives before I began this work. This does not mean that I was opposed to hospital birth or the associated technologies of childbirth. About six months into my fieldwork, I discovered I was pregnant with my second child. This became a tricky point for me in my research because I had to constantly relocate myself and my planned place of birth within the field depending on whom I was talking to. With midwives, my home birth was almost a given; in the hospital, I had to explain away my decision and emphasize my proximity to a tertiary hospital in case of emergency. Although I did not want to prescribe location or experience of birth for Indigenous women, I definitely thought that no mother should have to give birth in an unknown place without social support. I acknowledged my position and constantly negotiated this view within my research. I often found that I was not alone in this viewpoint. Despite the conflict over "safe" birthplaces, almost every actor— including obstetricians, nurses, and midwives—in my fieldwork agreed that the current system of evacuating women was broken and, indeed, needed fixing. With this in mind, I positioned myself as a "politically committed and morally engaged" anthropologist (Scheper-Hughes 409).

STUDYING MATERNAL EVACUATION IN MANITOBA

Maternal evacuation is not a new topic for academics, including anthropologists. In 1982, Lorna Guse wrote about the evacuation of pregnant women in Manitoba. Her research remains acutely relevant. Guse's descriptions of women's experiences in urban centre boarding homes in the 1980s could be observed and rewritten verbatim today. In medical anthropology, most well-known is the work of Patricia Kaufert and John O'Neill on evacuation policy and the Inuit of the northern region of Manitoba (427). Their seminal research on this topic began in the 1980s and became included in a number of important collections in medical anthropology, particularly the anthropology of reproduction (Ginsburg and Rapp; Lindenbaum and Lock 32). Subsequent research on maternal evacuation in Manitoba followed, mainly through graduate student dissertations (Hiebert; Eni; Phillips-Beck). Across Canada, numerous studies from various disciplines have focused on the multiple negative effects of relocation for birth, including "increased maternal newborn complications, increased post-partum depression and decreased breastfeeding rates" (Smith 143; see also: Klein et al. 120; Kornelson et al. 583). Maternal evacuation has also emerged as a research topic in Australia, where the system of health care and historical relationships with the Aboriginal population is similar to the Canadian context. (Kildea 387; Ireland et al. 634)

The current practice of maternal evacuation is the dominant way of managing the risk of childbirth for rural and remote Indigenous families. At the same time, however, midwives are now asking, "what are the risks of this practice?" In this way, risk takes on multiple meanings situated in specific times and spaces from particular historical, social, and cultural contexts. Sending women to a tertiary facility to deliver can be seen as an explicit practice of risk management governed by a notion of risk as 'manageable' through access to technologies and associated biomedical knowledge of Caesarean section operations and blood transfusions. Conversely, sending women to a tertiary facility to deliver alone, thus removing them from their social and familial context, can be also viewed as "risky."

In the case of maternal evacuation, one of the main concerns from previous studies is the lack of social support for women when they deliver. The premise of evacuation is based on a state requirement to provide access to primary care (i.e., pay for it). So in a way, the issue of evacuation is as much about economy as it is about the associated risks of childbirth.

HOSPITAL AS A RESEARCH SITE

As an ethnographer engaged in an explicit multisited field study, I understood the hospital where evacuated women give birth as a key site. In anthropological literature, the discourse of evacuation centres on the presence or absence of a tertiary hospital facility, yet this "space" of the dialogue is rarely critically examined. In the discourse of returning birth to the community, the notion of the hospital is often characterized as an oppressive institution that limits choice and exposes women to unnecessary intervention. From one federal doctor's perspective, the hospital is necessarily "a black box because you don't really know what happens [and what] goes on there." In other words, the hospital in the discourse of evacuation is an exclusive place, and knowledge of that place is limited to expert medical knowledge of the body and its treatment through technology. By framing the hospital in this way, the discourse automatically excludes everyone else from commenting on treatment or management of risk in these settings. From this perspective, the hospital is a bounded space of highly ordered, biomedical regulation: the "black box" in which the contents are "mysterious to the user" (Oxford). This view of the hospital presents significant limitations to the ethnographer working in its setting, as it may limit her ability to connect the goings-on of the hospital with the broader spaces and places in which the practice of maternal evacuation is present. Taking the opposite view, however, is also problematic: framing the hospital as a "microcosm of society" or "as continuations and reflections of everyday social space" may retract from acknowledging the space of the hospital as a "modernist institution of knowledge, governance, and improvement" (Street and Coleman 5). A solution is found in Alice Street and Simon Coleman's conception of the hospital as "simultaneously bounded and permeable, both sites of social control and spaces where alternative and transgressive social orders emerge and are contested" (4).

I conducted fieldwork in one of the two tertiary hospitals in Winnipeg, Manitoba. The hospital's labour and delivery ward is divided into two sections: Labour and Delivery (L&D) for high-risk patients and Labour, Delivery, Recovery, and Postpartum (LDRP) for low-risk patients. After birth, mother and baby are transferred to the Mother Child unit.

The hospital also has a history of providing care to evacuated women from the northern Manitoba, and various attempts to ameliorate the practice of evacuation have occurred over the years. Nurses and obstetricians in the urban centre hospital were diverse. Their role in monitoring and managing the care they provided was prescribed by their hospital protocols, and the boundaries of what they could and could not do were well defined. Most of the nurses and obstetricians I worked with were sympathetic to the struggles of the Indigenous women who had been evacuated. Upon hearing my thesis topic, one nurse commented, "Good. Maybe things will change."

<h2 style="text-align:center">IN THE HOSPITAL</h2>

The following three stories come from my experiences in LDRP and L&D of the hospital in Winnipeg. These stories are presented here as a way of seeing and understanding three women's experiences of delivering in this setting. In these stories, the women, Arlene, Nancy, and Cindy,[2] came from remote, northern communities to deliver. The stories show the range of risks created, realized, and subsequently managed in the hospital setting. Although hospital tries to manage the biomedical risks of pregnancy and birth, in Arlene's case, the lack of complications or intervention highlights the social risk of not having social support or family with her for her birth. In Nancy and Paul's story, the intervention of social services enters into the seemingly bounded space of the hospital by deciding who will care for the baby. In Cindy's case, her birth quickly became an emergency, and the hospital responded by performing an emergency Caesarean section. The hospital in these births become constructed in different ways: in Arlene's case, the hospital becomes an obstacle for her to experience birth in a familiar and supportive environment. For Nancy and Paul, the experience of birth in the hospital becomes conflated with the social interventions and decisions that have taken place outside of the hospital setting. For Cindy, the presence of the operating room becomes a key focus of her birth experience. These are dramatic moments, and within the discourse of evacuation, these stories could be seen as sitting in opposition to each other. However, the intricacies of their stories show that the hospital space is constantly negotiated and renegotiated by the women, their care providers, and the policymakers and outside actors who make decisions about who is present in the hospital and how they arrive and leave the building.

ARLENE'S STORY

Arlene has been in the L&D floor's triage for six hours. Triage is meant to be a place that women pass through on their way to one of the wings, not a place where a woman stays for long periods of time.

I go back through the curtain to the small space where Arlene has been labouring. She stands for each contraction and moves her hips in a circular motion.

"I didn't sleep last night," she says, "and I came in this morning." It is now just past three o'clock.

"They put this in me," she says, pointing to the IV stand attached to her through a needle in the back of her hand.

She gets another contraction, and I stand beside her with my hand on the small of her back. She begins to move her hips in circles again, and I tell her how that is a good thing to do to get the baby to move down.

Two nurses come into the room, and they say they are finally moving her to a room in LDRP. I carry her bags.

Once in LDRP, two nurses come and introduce themselves to Arlene. They are both in their mid-twenties: one is a nurse in LDRP, and the other is a student on one of her final shifts in the ward. They speak with us briefly and leave the room.

This is Arlene's second baby. She is from the far north and had her first baby in a northern community. This is her first time in Winnipeg.

Arlene is focused on her contractions and her breathing. They start to get more intense after a few more, and at one point, she begins to grunt a little—a tell-tale sign that she may be transitioning into the "pushing" phase. At this point, I get a bit worried that the nurses have not come in yet, so I make my way to the desk down the hallway and tell them I think that she is progressing fast and she is starting to want to push. They spring into action and come into the room with the birthing cart, with its sterilized tools wrapped up in blue paper. When the nurse checks her, she is only six centimetres dilated. Arlene has another contraction while the nurses are there, and I turn my focus away from the nurses, and back on her. I once again place my hand at the small of her back and begin to speak to her softly, telling her that she is doing great, and that her contraction is almost over.

A nurse tells Arlene about different options for pain relief. Arlene says she doesn't want anything. The nurse keeps talking and lists off her options: nitrous-oxide gas, fentanyl in her IV, or an epidural. Arlene asks if she can have the IV taken out, since it was put in by mistake. The nurse reads the chart and confirms, that yes, the IV was a mistake, but she decides not to remove it until after the birth, "just in case." The nurse reads something in the chart and turns to Arlene.

"The chart says you tested positive this week for a STD," the nurse asks her, "but it doesn't say which one. Do you know what you tested positive for?"

Arlene shakes her head no as another contraction begins.

From my point of view, sitting with Arlene during her labour and increasingly intense contractions, I think that things are going well. She is clearly progressing; her contractions are getting stronger and closer together; and she is making the signs that she is transitioning. I am surprised that they offer Arlene an epidural, since I don't really think that she will be in labour long enough to get it, but I am not a trained nurse, midwife, or doctor, so I keep all of these thoughts to myself.

Arlene is adamant that she does not want any kind of augmentation. She keeps saying it, and says no each time the nurse asks.

The nurses leave, and Arlene and I are again alone in the room. I stand next to her as she sits on the bed in between contractions. We hear a baby cry in another room: that brand new, first cry of a baby. It is one of the nicest parts of the labour and delivery floor.

"Huh," Arlene scoffs. "She's lucky."

We laugh at that, and I tell her that her baby will come soon too.

Time is funny when a woman is in labour. It either passes quickly or slowly. We have been in the room for an hour and a half, and it seems like no time has gone by. I go out to get Arlene water and ice from the machine outside her room, another blanket from the warmer, and stand with her during each contraction, with my hand on her back and talking softly into her ear.

As the minutes pass, she no longer wants to stand up during a contraction. Instead, she stays on the bed, moving her legs, trying to find something to push against. Even though not much time has passed, I really think that Arlene will have her baby soon, so I go out to the nursing desk again to find the two nurses assigned to Arlene. I tell them I think she is getting close. They don't jump up as quickly as they did the first time, seeing how I was wrong then, but they come into the room as Arlene has another contraction. I go to her again, and do the same thing I have been doing for each contraction. The contractions are getting longer and harder.

During the contraction, the nurse says, "Do you want nitrous oxide? It doesn't have a lasting effect."

Arlene shakes her head, but she cannot say more than that, since she is in the middle of a hard contraction.

"I will go get the nitrous for you," the nurse leaves the room.

"You don't have to take anything you don't want to," I tell Arlene when the nurse is gone.

She comes back quickly into the room, just as Arlene begins to contract again. The nurse comes to the bedside and thrusts a mask in her face. Arlene shakes her head no, so the nurse hands it to her to hold onto.

The other nurse checks her again, and she says that she is fully dilated and goes to call for the doctor. The nurses put Arlene's legs in the stirrups and get the bed ready for the delivery. The two nurses open the bed up so that the doctor can get close in-between her legs, and they attach a plastic bag to the bottom of the bed to catch any excess fluid from the birth. One unfolds the blue paper covering the birthing cart, and we wait for the doctor to arrive.

The doctor comes in with a resident, and they put on their gowns and masks. The resident doctor takes her position in-between Arlene's legs to deliver her baby. I am holding Arlene's leg in place, as it keeps falling off the stirrup.

With the next contraction, we all see the baby's head emerging. A few moments later, a little boy is born. Arlene smiles with relief. They take the baby to the OHIO (baby warmer) next to the bed, and check him to make sure that all is well. He is fine, and once the placenta is delivered, the resident and the doctor quickly leave the room. I realize I never even looked at them, and have no idea who they were.

Soon afterwards, while her baby boy is sleeping soundly under the warmer beside her, she asks if there is a telephone she can use. The nurse tells her no. She will have to wait until she is allowed to walk down the hall to the pay phone, and then she will need a calling card—which she doesn't have—to use it. I tell her I have a mobile that she could borrow. She takes it from me and dials a number.

Arlene, who up until this point has smiled and remained relatively calm throughout her labour and delivery, begins to dial a number on the phone. As soon as the person answers, a stream of words in her Indigenous language come pouring out of her, and she is crying. She talks for a few minutes and then quickly hangs up.

She looks at me. "Just one more?" she asks, holding up the phone.

"Yes, yes, of course," I say.

She dials again, and the same thing happens. She begins to speak her language, and tears begin to stream down her face.

Arlene wants to be closer to her baby, who is still quietly lying under the warmer. She moves to get up to see him, and I get up to help her as the IV gets tangled by the bedside. She says she hates that needle going into her and wants it taken out.

A new nurse comes in, and when she sees Arlene on her feet,

she quickly runs to her side and scolds her for getting out of bed. She turns to me and says, "Next time she does this, press the call button. It is difficult, especially with ones like these, who think they can do everything."

She says that she might as well change the sheets of the bed since Arlene is out of them. As she is changing them, she asks Arlene, "Do you smoke?"

Arlene says "yes," while she looks down and holds her baby's hand in the OHIO.

The nurse then begins to tell her about the dangers of smoking, and the effect it will have on her and her baby's health. In my head, I know these messages are important, yet I can't help but think how inappropriate it seems. Arlene is all by herself. She just gave birth to a little baby boy, and now she is being lectured about the dangers of smoking.

After the nurse leaves, Arlene picks up the baby and begins to breastfeed him. The nurse comes in and sees that Arlene is nursing, and quickly brings over a sheet of paper and a pencil. It is a chart to record when she feeds her baby and for how long. I mark down the first feeding on the chart for her.

Arlene gets sleepy, and so I tell her I will leave her to sleep with her baby. I say I will come back and visit tomorrow.

She smiles and replies, "I will be waiting for you."

NANCY AND PAUL'S STORY

"I don't hit my wife," he says to me, looking serious.

We are sitting in a small hospital room in the L&D ward of the hospital. His wife has just been induced, and her contractions are starting slowly. This comment may seem out of place, or maybe a bit strange to tell someone you don't know very well, but I get it. I nod in response. Violence in Indigenous communities is rampant, and violence against women is also common. Distinguishing himself as someone who does not do this is important for him, and I respect this. He gets out his mobile and shows me some photos of their one-year-old daughter. He tells me how cute she is with pride in his voice. They are excited for their new baby. They know they are going to have a little boy.

Nancy shifts uncomfortably in the bed. "Oh, I feel like I need to push," she says with a distressed look on her face. Then she stops and looks at us with a mischievous expression. "Naaahhhh!" she exclaims and breaks out into a huge grin, and we all laugh together at her joke.

I am glad that I can sit and laugh with Nancy and Paul while they wait for the arrival of their second baby. Their situation is a difficult one. Nancy's first baby is in care (meaning she has been taken by Child and Family Services and placed in another home, which, in this case, turns out to be Nancy's mother's), and this second baby will also go directly into her mother's care. There is a Birth Alert,[3] which specifies that apprehension will not take place directly after the baby has been born. It has been arranged with the social worker that Nancy and Paul can travel back to their home community with the baby, and he will be taken into care at that point. After this, Nancy and Paul have committed to attending a drug and alcohol treatment program.

The nurse explains to me that Nancy has some risk factors, which is why she is on the high-risk side of the labour floor. She is diabetic, and her baby seems big. The nurse keeps getting her to take her glucose readings by pricking her finger. Her sugar readings are low, so they give her some big glucose tablets to suck on. The nurse has a hard time reading her chart. It was faxed down by the community and, it is blurry. She can't tell if Nancy is GBS (Group B Strep) negative or positive. The nurse before her said they tried to get a hold of the nursing station in the community, but they did not answer the phone. The nurse goes to try and call them again.

I go back into the room and sit with them. They are speaking Cree to each other, so I just sit quietly with them. They explain to me that Paul has a doctor's appointment the next day for his eyes and they planned his appointment to coincide with the birth of their baby so that way he was also eligible for travel to the city and accommodation while he was there. I ask them about life up North, and how it is up there. They tell me about the summertime and travelling between communities on the river. "That's nice," Paul says, "but it is not a good place to live. Too much violence."

The nurse comes in to check her sugar level and to read her EFM (electronic fetal monitor). Nancy tries to tell her that the IV is dripping from her hand, but the nurse doesn't understand her quiet and broken English. I quickly explain what she is trying to say. The nurse then explains that they are using oxytocin to try and induce labour. Both Nancy and Paul turn directly to me to translate what the nurse has just said, not into Cree but into a way of speaking English that they can understand.

A friend from the boarding home comes to visit. She is a woman in her thirties in a wheelchair, with one leg missing. She is a diabetic. I leave the room so that they can visit together. When she leaves I go back in, and Nancy seems sad. She tells me she feels so bad for her friend, who is having a hard time. The mood sobers a bit. Nancy says she will try to sleep.

Her contractions are slowing down, after it looked as though things might have been moving along, and she decides to sleep for a while. Paul says he will watch a movie on the television they have wheeled into the room for him. I leave them to it and sit outside the room in the hall, and speak with the nurse attending to them. She tells me that she found out what Nancy is addicted to. She drinks alcohol and sniffs gasoline.

When speaking of the Indigenous women who come here to deliver, the nurse remarks that "a lot of them come here; as a culture, they are usually very accommodating. Like this lady [Nancy], she is just taking it in her stride. A lot of them are very good natured. And a lot of them do have a close family network, so they seem to do okay."

It is getting late in the afternoon, and I tell Nancy and Paul that I am going to go home for the day. Her labour is slowing down, and they are upping the rates of oxytocin with no change in either the length or the frequency of contractions. I say goodbye, and I will see them tomorrow.

The next day, I am walking through the lobby of the hospital when I hear someone shout "There she is!" I look over to other side of the room and see Nancy and Paul walking toward me. They are coming in from going for a cigarette at the front of the building. She tells me she had her baby last night at two in the morning, and I follow them up to their room in the postpartum wing to meet him. We find the baby at the nurse's desk in a bassinet, where the nurses have agreed to watch him while they went outside, and we roll him down the hall to their room that they share with three other couples. It is a tight squeeze to fit the bassinet beside the bed, and Paul and Nancy sit down to tell me that everything went well with the birth of their son. Nancy tells me she just arranged their flights back for the next day. Paul went for his eye appointment that morning, so they are both ready to go home. The baby sleeps peacefully as I hold him. He is beautiful, and I tell them that I am so happy for them. We don't talk about what is going to happen next. We just sit quietly for a long time and watch this new little baby sleep.

CINDY'S STORY

I can hear Cindy moaning as the shift changes in the main hallway of the L&D. The nurses are crowded around a large, flat screen television mounted on the wall. The nurses coming off nights and the nurses beginning days discuss the updates of each patient. The NIC (nurse in charge) reads down the list, adding small comments to what is already written there—mostly stuff about the number of pregnancies, status of Group B Strep (positive or negative), rubella, centimetres dilated, and the amounts and types of medications the women are currently on. I can't hear or understand most of it.

A young nurse in her early twenties is going to be Cindy's nurse for the day shift. Cindy's moans are audible in the hall, and nurses exchange amused glances each time she cries out. I follow the nurse into her room.

It is dark; she is on the bed with a nitrous oxide mask covering her face. Her mother is curled up and sleeping in the chair in the corner with her coat over her head. Cindy is nineteen years old, and she is from a northern, remote community.

The tracings are pumping out heartbeats and contractions. The contractions are not adequate, according to the nurse as she unfolds the stack of paper. The nitrous oxide tank is empty, and a nurse goes to get another one. Cindy has had a failed epidural, and right now, her pain relief consists of fentanyl being administered through her IV, and the nitrous oxide gas. She is struggling, though, and cries out during each contraction.

The nurse leaves to get more medication from the dispensary. I find a stool and sit down next to Cindy. With each contraction, Cynthia tenses, moans, and cries out. I put my hand on her leg and say, "deep breaths," and "it's almost over, and then you can rest," even though I have no idea where she is at or what is happening with her labour.

Cindy gulps into the nitrous oxide mask.

The nurses come in again and look at the fetal monitor. They take her temperature. Cindy is hooked up to an IV stand, with an internal fetal monitor connected through a wire inside her vagina, a catheter, a blood pressure cuff on her ankle, and a finger clip. With the next contraction, Cindy cries out again. The nurse holds her hand and rubs her leg. She walks back to the counter edge to prepare the fentanyl to be injected into Cindy's IV. Cindy cries out again.

"Calm down," the nurse says, "You can do this. You are in control here."

When the nurse walks out, I lean over to Cindy and say, "Don't worry, you can make as much noise as you want; you are the one in labour." I hold Cindy's hand during every contraction. I talk to her in a low, calm voice, and I tell her she is doing a great job.

The nurse comes in with a foil package with three Tylenol. Cindy has a fever, and they are going to try and bring it down. Cindy thinks that they are for pain relief, and asks if the Tylenol are T3s (paracetamol with codeine added). They say no. They are only regular strength, and Cindy cries, "these aren't going to help me at all!" They explain that it is for her fever, not for pain relief.

"The baby's heart rate is really high," the nurse whispers to me.

The resident doctor comes in to assess Cindy. She looks at her chart and her tracings. They are going to need to do a C-section. They are going to call Cindy's obstetrician and see what he says. He tells them to wait until he gets there. The baby's heart rate is rising, and I can feel the tension of the nursing staff rising along with it. I sit with Cindy and continue to hold her hand. She squeezes my hand as hard as she can during contractions, and I am reminded of all those sitcoms on television in which the father's hand gets crushed by the mom in labour. It hurts, but I don't really mind. I am focusing on Cindy, and helping her through her contractions in the only way I know how—by sitting with her and telling her she is going to be okay.

The nurses come rushing in and out. They check her temperature again and make notes in the charts. The resident comes in again and looks at the EFM. The baby's heart rate is racing. She goes out again, and finds that all of the operating rooms are currently occupied with other C-sections taking place. The obstetrician arrives, and suddenly a flurry of activity begins.

An emergency C-section is deemed necessary. The nurses run to set up; I remain seated with Cindy. Her mom gets out of the bed as another nurse explains to them that Cindy is going to have a C-section, but that the mother can't come in, since it is an emergency situation. I tell Cindy's mother I will come out of the operating room as soon as I can and let her know how things are going. The anesthesiologist comes into the room as asks me who I am. I say an "anthropology student," and he tells me to wear my ID on my green scrubs shirt pocket, instead of clipped to the bottom of my shirt. I quickly move my ID, which happens to be my University of Sussex student card slipped into a plastic card holder, and get out of his way. We begin to wheel Cindy out of the room, and the NIC yells over to me, "Rachel, take her temperature quickly, will you?" I immediately say, "I can't." I am not a nurse or a medical student, and it is at times like these that I wish I had continued with my midwifery degree so that I could have some practical skills to contribute to this scenario. We are rushing down the hallway, from the darkness of the room to the bright fluorescent glow of the main halls of the labour floor. At the door to the operating rooms, I grab a surgical cap and mask from the dispensary box on the wall, and quickly put them on as I walk alongside Cindy. She is still crying and moaning. For a second time, I feel as if I am in a television show, except this time, it is one of those hospital dramas.

In the operating room, I wonder if I am going to be okay. I have never been in surgery before, and I wonder how I will react. My main focus is not to get in anyone's way as people are rushing around. The anesthesiologist tells me not to touch anything with the blue paper because that is sterile. Now that he knows I am a student, anthropology or otherwise, he is happy to explain these things to me. They are going to put Cindy to sleep, since the previous attempts at giving her an epidural failed.

"Rachel, move up here and hold her hand," the nurse says. They are transferring her to the operating table, and Cindy begins to cry in huge sobs. I move forward and hold her hand again.

"Stay there with her," the nurse advises. I move aside and hold Cindy's other hand, as they place the mask on her face. They put up a curtain only halfway, and I can see over it and watch them prep Cindy's belly.

The neonatologists come in and stand along the wall next to the OHIO, getting ready for the baby. A student comes into the operating room to assist the obstetrician. The obstetrician slowly makes the incision, and at the crucial moment of getting the baby out, he yells at the student to push on the fundus. She stares at him blankly and doesn't move.

"The fundus, the fundus," he repeats sternly.

I want to reach over the curtain and press on the top of Cindy's stomach— the fundus—but I know it isn't my place. The anaesthesiologist leans over and does it instead.

Once the baby is out, the neonatal doctors grab it immediately and place it on the OHIO. They hold a tube of oxygen up to its face; they lift up the baby's arms and move its lifeless body, trying to get the baby to breathe. Finally, they have to intubate the baby. This means a tube is put down the baby's throat. The obstetrician is methodically finishing the operation, closing up the uterus and the layers above it, but his eyes keep going back to the baby, watching it. It is a little girl.

"How is that baby doing, doctor?" he asks the neonatologist.

They manage to take the tube out, and the baby is breathing on her own. They bundle her off to the NICU (the Neonatal Intensive Care Unit), and I find out later that the baby had to be intubated again once she arrived there.

I realize I have been holding Cindy's hand tightly the whole time and haven't let go.

DISCUSSION

In a discussion of returning birth to an Indigenous community, Arlene is a prime candidate to stay in the community for delivery:

she had a normal first pregnancy and delivery, and had no risk factors that would necessitate her being in a tertiary facility.

From the nurses' and obstetrician's point of view, the hospital is still the safest place to give birth; however, when you add the iatrogenic effects of evacuation as risk management, the argument for returning birth outweighs the chances of an adverse birth outcome. From the perspective of biomedical risk, Arlene's birth was uneventful. Yet her birth highlights the social isolation of a woman who was sent away to have her baby. The first contact she had with someone familiar was filled with emotion and tears, which was something she never revealed to me or the other nurses during her labour and delivery.

Nancy and Paul's story shows how outside forces, such as Child and Family Services and medical travel, are active participants in the construction of how childbirth is experienced by the new parents. The influence of these outside agencies show how permeable the boundaries of the hospital actually are, and how researchers need to look at the broader systems and structures that make up maternal evacuation to fully understand the broad range of factors that influence the practice.

Cindy's experience of birth, an emergency, is often given as a reason not to deliver away from a facility without Caesarean capability. However, this story does not contribute to the polarizing discourse around evacuation. Rather, acknowledging the presence of risks and then negotiating them in conjunction with other kinds of risks emerges as a key conclusion. As Carol Couchie, an Aboriginal midwife, explained to me:

> When everything goes wrong and people are really sick, and women are at risk of dying or babies dying, like the sort of bad stuff that people talk about—what happens at birth—it's the obstetricians that care for those people, obstetricians and paediatricians. So midwives can't do their work in a modern context without them, we know it. But obstetricians can't do their job well without us.

What both Cindy's and Arlene's births show is how little room exists for negotiating one's experience of birth within the hospital setting: the nurse told Cindy that she was in control, but Cindy was hooked up to machinery both through IVs and vaginal monitors with no way of moving around, much less feeling in control of the situation; likewise, Arlene was given an IV that inhibited her movement and experience of labour and birth as she tried to manoeuvre in the hospital room. The routinization of monitoring and administering interventions in the hospital both mitigated and produced risk in this setting. Although in the case of Cindy the risks of fetal and maternal death were given precedence and overtly negotiated, the nurse's insistence that she was in control was in response to mitigating a different kind of risk—one that is grounded in the notion of emotional safety. Arlene's decision to move around after birth and to breastfeed without assistance or guidance was also construed as a threat to her own safety in the hospital setting. She was to be watched closer because she "thinks she can do everything."

What all birth stories show is the little available to negotiate one's experience of birth within the hospital setting. Negotiation of social risks by women and their families was addressed throughout the process of evacuation by the women and their families themselves. This chapter has shown that the biomedical risks of childbirth were consistently given precedence over the mitigation of social risks by the healthcare system and policymakers. This coincides with Alice Hamilton's observation that biomedical maternity care "continues to place objective medical risk over women's subjectively defined risks, leaving women to cope with their own risk in their own ways" (73). However, in the case of maternal evacuation, these social risks are now being addressed by the growing support for Indigenous midwifery and the return of birth to communities. Until then, I want to honour and acknowledge the women I had the privilege of spending time with in the hospital setting. I also want to acknowledge those Indigenous women who I am sure are in the hospital now, birthing alone, as I write and continue to hope for change.

ENDNOTES

[1]This research was passed through the Assembly of Manitoba Chiefs

Health Information Research Committee Ethics, Health Research Ethics Board of the University of Manitoba, the Norway House Cree Nation Research Committee, the hospital's Research Ethics Committee, and the ethics process at the University of Sussex.
[2]Pseudonyms are used for the women in these stories.
[3]A Birth Alert is issued by Child and Family Services of Manitoba and applies "to expectant mothers considered by agencies to be high risk in relation to the care they will provide for their newborn infant. The practice in Manitoba is to issue alerts to track and locate these high-risk expectant mothers" (Government of Manitoba 1).

WORKS CITED

Couchie, Carol. Personal interview. 15 Jan. 2010.

Eni, Rachel. "An Articulation of the Standpoint of Peer Support Workers to Inform Childbearing Program Supports in Manitoba First Nation communities: Institutional Ethnography as De-colonizing Methodology." Dissertation, University of Manitoba, 2005.

Ginsburg, F.D., and R. Rapp, editors. *Conceiving the New World Order: The Global Politics of Reproduction.* University of California Press, 2005.

Guse, L. "Maternal Evacuation: A Study of the Experiences of Northern Manitoba Native Women." Dissertation University of Manitoba, 1982.

Hamilton, A.B. "The Vital Conjuncture of Methamphetamine-Involved Pregnancy: Objective Risks and Subjective Realities." *Risk, Reproduction, and Narratives of Experience,* edited by L. Fordyce and A. Maraësa, Vanderbilt University Press, 2012, pp. 59-77.

Hiebert, S. "NCN Otinawasuwuk (receivers of children): Taking control of birth in Nisichawayasihk Cree Nation." Dissertation, University of Manitoba, 2003.

Ireland, S., et al. "Niyith Nniyith Watmam (the Quiet Story): Exploring the Experiences of Aboriginal Women Who Give Birth in Their Remote Community." *Midwifery,* vol. 27, no. 5, 2011, pp. 634-41.

Kaufert, P., and J.D. O'Neil. "Cooptation and Control: The Reconstruction of Inuit Birth." *Medical Anthropology Quarterly*, vol. 4, no. 4, 1990, 427-42.

Kaufert, P., and J.D. O'Neil. "Analysis of a Dialogue on Risks in Childbirth: Clinicians, Epidemiologists, and Inuit Women." *Knowledge, Power, and Practice: The Anthropology of Medicine and Everyday Life*, edited by S. Lindenbaum and M.M. Lock, University of California, 1993, pp. 32.

Kildea, S. "Risky business: Contested Knowledge over Safe Birthing Services for Aboriginal Women." *Health Sociology Review*, vol. 15, no. 4, 2006, pp. 387-96.

Klein, M.C., et al. "Loss of Maternity Care: The Cascade of Unforeseen Dangers." *Canadian Journal of Rural Medicine*, vol. 7, no. 2, 2002, pp. 120-21.

Kornelsen, J., et al. "Geographic Induction of Rural Parturient Women: Is It Time for a Protocol?" *Journal of Obstetrics and Gynecology Canada*, vol. 29, no. 7, 2007, pp. 583-85.

Lindenbaum, S., and M.M. Lock, editors. *Knowledge, Power, and Practice: The Anthropology of Medicine and Everyday Life.* University of California Press, 1993.

"Black Box." *Oxford Dictionaries*, 2012, en.oxforddictionaries.com/definition/black_box. Accessed 27 Aug. 2017.

Phillips-Beck, W. "Development of a Framework of Improved Childbirth Care for First Nation Women in Manitoba: A First Nation Family Centred Approach." Dissertation, University of Manitoba, 2010.

Scheper-Hughes, N. "The Primacy of the Ethical: Propositions for a Militant Anthropology." *Current Anthropology*, vol. 36, no. 3, 1995, pp. 409-40.

Smith, D. "Maternal-Child Health Care in Aboriginal Communities." *Canadian Journal of Nursing Research*, vol. 35, no. 2, 2003, pp. 143-52.

Street, A., and S. Coleman. "Introduction: Real and Imagined Spaces." *Space and Culture*, vol. 15, no. 1, 2012, pp. 4-17.

6.
Honouring Our Ancestors

Reclaiming the Power of Māori Maternities

NAOMI SIMMONDS, RAUKAWA, NGĀTI HURI

Ancestors whisper and chorus
Your whakapapa grows with you.
(Kahukiwa and Potiki 83)

MĀORI[1] MATERNAL KNOWLEDGES are intimately tied to ancestors, to ancestral knowledges, and to *whenua* (land).[2] *Iwi* (tribes), *hapū* (smaller tribal groupings), and *whānau* (families)[3] have their own maternal knowledges, which are woven into their cosmologies, histories, songs, carvings, place names, chants, and incantations. These knowledges, though spatially and temporally specific, speak to the sanctity of the maternal body, the power and prestige of women's reproductive capabilities, and the empowering collective approach to raising children. Māori knowledges pertaining to pregnancy, childbirth, and parenting were imparted generation to generation as they were lived, embodied and emplaced by our ancestors, sustaining the sacred and empowering approach to maternities within our communities.

This chapter considers the challenges and possibilities of reclaiming Māori maternal knowledges and their associated practices and ceremonies for Māori women and whānau in contemporary *Aotearoa*-New Zealand. Three key themes frame this chapter. First, I consider the ways in which colonialism has served to silence Māori maternal knowledges to such an extent that whānau are left trying to find meaning in the voices, knowledges, and advices of others. Indigenous women are largely birthing within Western ideologies and institutions that do not adequately provide for Indigenous ways of being and birthing. The chapter then considers the ways in which women and whānau are reclaiming ancient knowledges and practices in new and contemporary ways. I seek to illustrate the ways in which traditional practices and ritual customs have the potential to transform and empower individual and collective experiences of birth and afterbirth. The chapter ends with arguing that Indigenous maternities, Māori maternities, are an important site of decolonization. Reclaiming the messages and embodied practices left to us by our ancestors can provide an empowering collective approach to pregnancy, birth, and afterbirth, and can facilitate a "decolonized pathway" (Simpson 28) into and through the world for our children and for generations to come.

MĀORI MATERNITIES

Māori maternities have been largely represented and enacted through the creative arts, tribal-based projects, and in the lived experiences of women and whānau. Many creative artists have dedicated their works to tracing what pregnancy, birth, and mothering has been like for Māori women throughout history (Grace; Kahukiwa and Potiki). These women and many others are making vital contributions to Māori maternities. Studies of Māori maternities within the academy, however, are relatively scarce. There are of course exceptions, all of which are important precursors to this research (Gabel; Murphy; Mikaere, *Balance Destroyed*).

This chapter is based on my PhD research, which seeks to add to the growing body of literature pertaining to Māori maternities (Simmonds). The research sought to understand the contemporary experiences of birth for women and whānau in Aotearoa. A total of thirty-two women and whānau participated in the research—through interviews, *wānanga* (group interviews), diary writing, and participation in an online forum. The narratives shared in the research, some of which are presented in this chapter, illustrate the inextricability of the maternal body from land, language, and spirituality. Women in the research also discussed the effects of colonial impositions on their present day understandings and experiences of pregnancy and birth. What the research highlights, however, is that Indigenous women have richly textured and colourfully woven birthing experiences, which demonstrate how reclaiming our ancestors' maternal knowledges and practices can transform the spaces—discursive, symbolic, and material—of birth for women and their whānau.

SILENCING THE POWER OF MĀORI MATERNITIES

Colonialism has employed many mechanisms used to silence, fragment, and marginalize Māori maternal knowledges and practices (Mikaere, *Balance Destroyed*). Colonial retellings of our cosmologies, histories, and stories consigned Māori knowledges, specifically maternal knowledges, to the realm of myth or superstition, or completely erased them altogether. Representations of our ancestresses were distorted and their power negated. Furthermore, the Aotearoa's legislative landscape has also served to marginalize Māori maternities through the forced hospitalization of birth (and subsequent sterilization and surveillance), the disenfranchisement of our *tohunga* (spiritual experts), and traditional birth attendants (through the 1904 Midwifery Registration Act and the 1907 Tohunga Suppression Act). Add to this the physical dislocation from tribal lands, land confiscation, spiritual disempowerment through Christianity, economic hardship and poverty, and the marginalization of our language, and it is not surprising that colonialism has transformed the spaces of birth in Aotearoa-New Zealand.

As a result, pregnancy and childbirth knowledges have largely transferred from the auspices of whānau, hapū, traditional birth attendants, and spiritual experts to registered midwives (most of whom are non-Māori) or doctors (most of whom are non-Māori men). The state's drive to medicalize and hospitalize birth has led to Māori birthing becoming almost completely institutionalized; by 1967, for example, 95 percent of Māori births occurred in hospitals (Donley 122). Despite the natural and home birth movements of the 1980s, this has largely remained unchanged: 87 percent of all births in New Zealand happen in a tertiary or secondary maternity facility (New Zealand, Ministry of Health).[4]

I argue a political imperative exists to keep birth located within institutionalized spaces. Confining birth to the hospital setting contains a powerful political message that can limit how, when, and where women birth, and can define who may be involved in birth. Ani Mikaere makes a similar point:

> Control over the process was completely in the hands of medical professionals, the doctors and the hospital staff. Husbands were not present, nor it seems, were other members of the whānau. The woman was completely isolated from her whānau and surrounded by strangers. There was no choice of location, nor of method. She was expected to lie on her back with her feet in stirrups and endure regular internal examinations without protest. There was no question of karakia [incantations] to Hineteiwaiwa [deity presiding over birth], for hospitals were about science, not superstition. And when the placenta eventually came away, it was borne off to the hospital incinerators without question. (*Balance Destroyed*, 92-93)

Māori women are not alone in experiencing the forced transition of birth to the hospital and the institutionalization of birth. Anishinaabeg scholar Leanne Simpson argues for many Indigenous women in Canada and elsewhere "colonialism has ... for the most part stolen the pregnancy and birth ceremony from our women, undermining our sovereignty and our knowledge and our power as women" (31). In New Zealand, after some 170 years of imposed systems, ideologies, and practices (for other Indigenous communities around the world this time period is much longer), the reality today is that for a number of whanau, knowing and learning as our ancestors did is not always possible. Instead, many Māori women are left to try and find meaning in the words of others.

The fragmentation and silencing of traditional knowledges has increasingly relied on "professional" or "expert" advice pertaining to pregnancy and childbirth. Although midwifery in New Zealand focuses on learning and understanding maternal processes through story sharing with other women, by and large, authority about maternal matters still sits firmly within institutions. Antenatal education, midwives, doctors, books, and state-produced pamphlets and websites have become the primary sources of information, particularly for first-time mothers. These dominant narratives and knowledges are not neutral or impartial; rather, they are produced in a monocultural framework of maternity care that fails to adequately provide for Mvori or Indigenous maternities (Kenney). These knowledges and how they are taught can leave Māori women and whānau feeling uncomfortable, marginal, or even invisible.

In the Māori language, the word "whenua" means both land and placenta. The Māori cultural practice of returning the placenta to the earth by burying it is a significant one for both birthing practices and establishing a "homeplace" for the newborn child. This particular practice is one that has run the gamut of colonial impositions, and as such, a number of women in my PhD research felt that there was still a limited understanding by many maternity practitioners of the importance of this practice. One such mother reflected on the lack of cultural understanding of this practice at a mainstream antenatal class. In her diary, she wrote about feeling confronted and upset:

> I remember at antenatal classes, we looked like the only Māori couple and the teacher was going "you know some people decide to keep the placenta" ... someone else in the group said "do people really do that? That's so gross!" ... Of all the conversations at antenatal classes, of all the things we were "taught" I remember this statement the most ... I immediately felt offended ... it almost made me cry, it made me mad, sad—a lot of things. It was like she was speaking to my baby saying that the whenua [placenta] that has nourished you for nine months, has given you life, is "gross." It hurt my feelings.

The space of mainstream antenatal class for this mother and her husband felt culturally unsafe, and she experienced feelings of shame and embarrassment. Because of this encounter, she subsequently became silent about other cultural practices they were planning for the birth of their son. Fiona Cram and Linda Smith point out that a number of health checks and medical procedures, such as cervical smears and internal examinations during pregnancy, for Māori women are culturally and physically invasive and that "cultural safety" is not always understood. In other words "the cultural mores of modesty are not understood by, or even recognized by most health professionals and especially doctors" (Cartwright Inquiry 115). Therefore, it is not simply the biophysical safety of women's maternal bodies that needs to be considered. Providing culturally appropriate maternity services is necessary if Māori women are to feel supported and respected in their pregnancy and birthing experiences.

This silence, or silencing, was not uncommon among whānau I spoke with. A number of our *kuia* (female Elders) reflected on how little their mothers and grandmothers spoke of their own birthing experiences. When one of the participants asked her own Elders why this was the case, they responded: "The nannies aren't talking about it because they all got made to feel that a Māori birthing process wasn't as good as a Pākehā [non-Māori New Zealander] one." What these narratives reinforce is that hegemonic maternity knowledges and practices are imbued with culturally constructed discourses about the right way to birth. As a result, other ways of birthing and parenting can become silenced.

The hurt and marginalization experienced by previous generations is often felt and embodied by women today. The silence, hurt, and shame is not always confined to the individual but can be produced and reproduced in the experiences of women across generations. We continue to live with, and are shaped by, the silence (both contemporary and historical) that surrounds Māori and Indigenous maternities. Māori women, however, are not passive victims of this silence. They actively shape silence. In fact, some women choose silence as a strategy of resistance. For example, women choose not to participate in mainstream antenatal education; they only reveal bits of information to others about birth plans and perform ceremony in ways that are unheard. These are powerful acts of resistance toward protecting Māori knowledges in spaces that fail to recognize their value.

Not only are women today giving form to silence, but they are also actively working to break it. For many, the experience of birth has prompted them to do so. Hoping that their children will not have to struggle against colonialism, in the same ways that they have, many whānau are beginning to voice what previously unspoken. For many, their *karanga* (call) to their children is becoming so loud that they shatter the silence and reclaim their power and knowledge as women, as Māori women.

RECLAIMING OUR *TIKANGA*, RECLAIMING OURSELVES

Mikaere describes "tikanga" as "the practical expression of a philosophy that is founded in the experience of our tūpuna [ancestors], and has been adapted over time in the light of successive generations' experience and circumstances" (*Colonising Myths* 25). Sometimes understood as customs, traditions, practices, or ethical behaviour, "tikanga," Mikaere argues, is the practical application of values embedded in our worldviews and knowledges that is pivotal to our identity, community, and to our survival as Māori. She writes that it is "imperative to treasure those physical manifestations and expressions of ancestors that connect us to our origins and enable us to project ourselves with confidence into the future" (298).

As the narratives in the previous section suggest, despite the impacts of colonialism, a number of women and whānau are reclaiming traditional knowledges and associated tikanga pertaining to pregnancy and childbirth, such as the return of the placenta to the earth. Indeed all of the stories and experiences shared in my research have made me confident that Māori maternal tikanga continue to exist and inform the birthing experiences of women and whānau today. It is my contention that colonialism, though significant in our lived realities, should not be the defining feature of Māori women's maternity experiences and we must look beyond colonialism to those stories, concepts, and practices celebrating maternities from a uniquely Māori perspective.

Women vary in their use of birthing tikanga and traditions; some perform a multiplicity of tikanga. One mother explained as follows.

We used muka [softened flax fibre] to tie the pito [umbilical cord] and greenstone to cut the cord and made ipu whenua [container for the placenta]. My boy went straight into a wahakura (woven basket) for sleeping. I went down to my sister's antenatal class which was on the marae ... at the

class we made muka [softened flax fibre]. We made our
ipu whenua [container for the placenta] ... I got a friend
of mine to cut the cord with greenstone. It makes sense
because that's how they would have done it back in the
day as well. All our terminology, as far as we would refer
to our body parts and our baby and processes were all in
Māori; little waiata [songs] and things like that ... Also, it
wasn't just me; the whānau were on board, and they would
actually just get things and do things.

The use of tikanga for this woman and her whānau was both
material and symbolic. She highlights the role her whānau took in
reclaiming of tikanga for her son's birth. The collective responsibility
in recovering Indigenous maternities is pivotal if *wāhine* (women)
are to feel empowered in their birthing experiences. This responsibility must be shared by many. The potential for overburdening
women who are in the throes of caring for new babies and infants
is very real. Therefore, we must encourage the wider collective,
the maternity practitioners, and the wider sociopolitical context
in supporting women and whānau to engage in this important and
potentially transformative work.

Furthermore, feeling that tikanga must be enacted in a particular
way is often connected to notions of authenticity, which tend to
fix tradition and tikanga in a specific place and time. For example,
not all women had whānau to assist them; some also faced other
challenges in reclaiming particular tikanga. One woman in her early
thirties explained that she did not have the time, and sometimes
the confidence, to incorporate all of the things she wanted into her
birthing experience: "I really wanted to make muka [softened flax
fibre] to tie the cord. I wish I would have been a lot more confident to do those sorts of things. I wish I was a lot more confident
and organised. Pregnancy goes fast." The conceptualization and
performance of tikanga and tradition, therefore, must be fluid and
dynamic if it is to account for the diversity of women and whānau
experiences of birth and afterbirth today. Although tikanga can
provide a blueprint created by our tūpuna, it is not, and should
not, be rigid or fixed in its expression. The underlying values and
philosophy of tikanga reminds us of the purpose and intent of the

embodied practice, which should always be remembered. As Ani Mikaere observes:

> It was our tūpuna who developed it, confident in the ex-pectation that the generations to come would continue to utilise and adapt it to meet their needs. They had faith in the theory of existence that they inherited from their tūpu-na. They were secure in their knowledge that the tikanga they implemented as a practical expression of that theory was capable of dealing with life's daily challenges ... we are the inheritors of that tradition. (*Colonising Myths*, 18)

WHENUA KI TE WHENUA

As mentioned previously, one of the traditions that we have inherited is the practice of "whenua ki te whenua"—returning the placenta to the earth. This tikanga has seen a particular resurgence in recent decades. Its importance can be found in the duality of the word "whenua," at once meaning land and placenta. The merging of mother, child, and *Papatūānuku* [Earth Mother] through this practice creates a reciprocal relationship of nurturance and sustenance. At the same time, burying the whenua can serve to establish a sense of home or belonging for a child and is, therefore, particularly important to the wider spatial politics of afterbirth.

The importance of returning the whenua is such that one home-birth midwife judged her performance as a midwife not only on the safe delivery of babies but on the return of the afterbirth to the earth: It's not how many babies I've delivered at home ... it's how many whenua have gone back to Papatūānuku, and it's 100 percent, and I think that's what makes me proud of my mahi [work]." Sadly, institutionalized spaces have not always provided for this tikanga. The refusal to return the placenta to whānau when women moved into hospitals to birth is perhaps one of the most visceral attacks on Māori maternities. Hospital policy from the mid-nineteenth century until approximately the late 1980s was that the whenua would be burned or thrown in the rubbish. The ritual care that Māori gave to the afterbirth was completely disregarded by institutions and non-Māori practitioners, the effects of which are difficult to fully comprehend.

Traditionally whenua would be returned to a special place, usually on the tribal lands of either mother or father (Makereti). In some cases, the whenua may have been buried at a boundary marker between tribal lands. Some evidence suggests that they were buried under a special tree or stone. For some whanau, the whenua would be buried in their tribal or familial *urupā* (burial ground).

As whānau became increasingly mobile and urbanized, where whenua are being buried has changed and continues to change. For example, some women or whānau make a long trip to return their baby's placenta to their tribal lands. One woman explained the twelve-hour round trip that her family makes to return the placenta to her tribal lands:

> We take baby's placenta up north. I know some people put it in the freezer, but our family always put it straight into the ground. We don't have any gourds or any weaving baskets; we just put it straight in. We're a no frills people. It just sort of sat in the boot for the night and then mum and dad went up north on the Tuesday and took her whenua home and buried it at our urupā by my grandfather's grave. Then you have a cup of tea and come home. It sounds crazy. It's a long trip but that's the beauty of it though. For us, it is a matter of time. We do it as soon as we can; so that's where they're from ... that is why we do it, so that people can never say "oh you don't belong here." I think it's because we're not home so you want to get them home as soon as we can.

For some women, however, this is not possible. Some women cannot return home immediately or are unlikely to return in the foreseeable future. For example, some women buried the whenua in a potted plant until such a time that they could return home. On an online forum discussion, one women write the following:

> My mum went and bought a miniature Kowhai tree for Okaire, it is placed in this pot which is a bluey colour to

represent his water birth. We chose a kowhai tree as they are really common up the east coast and we love them because when they bloom it means the kinas [sea urchins] are fat. Also chose to bury baby's whenua in this pot because I want to wait till we have time to go back to our land up the coast and bury it there.

Another woman kept the whenua at home for some time:

He [husband] didn't want them [hospital staff] putting bubba's whenua into the fridge with the other stuff. So I never saw the whenua at all because I had Caesareans, and they just took them away put it into the hue [gourd] and then closed it up; oh and we had it for quite a while; it didn't have a smell or anything, but we kept it until we could go back home and bury it. We just kept it at home in the lounge, sort of close to us.

For some women, at the time of the interview they had yet to determine where that "homeplace" will be. One woman wrote the following in her diary: "We still haven't buried our baby's whenua yet—we have discussed a location for it but just haven't done it yet. In the meantime, her whenua is sitting in our lounge, under the couch. We're probably breaking a rule or two keeping it there, not burying it just yet—but at least it's not in the fridge or deep freeze!"

Within Māori tikanga, putting the whenua with food is considered culturally inappropriate. The whenua is considered *tapu* (sacred), and food is used to *whakanoa* (remove the tapu); hence, they need to be separated.[5] This has not always been possible, and in the early days, hospitals would store the placenta in ice cream containers or plastic bags in fridges and freezers alongside food. Although this has largely changed, these narratives do highlight that Māori birthing tikanga afford an ethics of care to the afterbirth not always understood by those charged with caring for pregnant and birthing women and whānau.

The way whānau perform this tikanga is diverse and evolving, changing to meet their contemporary realities and needs. What does not seem to have changed is the intent and function of the tikanga. Where and when whānau bury the whenua are still important considerations; furthermore, the use of *ipu whenua* (container to hold the placenta) is being revitalized in new and creative ways. The disconnection created by colonialism means that for some "returning to one's native place is not an option for everyone but that does not mean that meaningful traditions and values that may have been part of their past cannot be integrated into homeplace wherever they make it" (hooks 213).

My research has found that honouring our ancestors through reclaiming, and at times recreating, traditional practices can instill women and whānau with a sense of confidence in their abilities to carry, birth, and mother as well as provide them with a range of coping strategies and support. Underlying the outer manifestations of traditional practices are values at the heart of Māori maternities. The sacredness of life and of women's bodies—the collective approach to raising children, and the centrality of children to the wellbeing of our communities, to name a few—must not be forgotten. Reclaiming tikanga is tied to reclaiming our knowledges, reclaiming confidence in our own traditions, and ultimately reclaiming ourselves—our sense of identity, culture, and belonging.

DECOLONIZING MATERNITIES

All Māori women are involved in a decolonizing politics, whether knowingly or not. Māori women and whānau negotiate the complexities of the intersecting oppressions of colonialism and patriarchy (and often class-based and homophobic oppressions) on a daily basis. In my research, I have been overwhelmed by the commonality that the wāhine share. Despite multiple oppressions and hardships, they continue to uphold and honour the maternal traditions and knowledges of our ancestors. This research—as well as other local research (Gabel; Mikaere; Murphy; Stephenson et.al.) and international research (Anderson; Lavell-Harvard and Corbiere Lavell; Simpson)—shows that Indigenous maternal knowledges do exist and are embodied, enacted, and performed in multiple ways.

For many of the women in this research, their maternal journey was the impetus for them to (re)claim a politics of self, of motherhood, and of culture that may not have been a focus otherwise. In fact, many women felt that the act of giving birth itself is an empowering and transformative experience. For example, one mother in her thirties said the following:

> Even though birth didn't go as planned [she had to have a Caesarean section], I'm still proud of and really thankful of my body for doing its job. This journey has definitely made me feel so much stronger and have faith in myself, my culture, and beliefs. The high when my baby finally was in my arms was amazing. I was more elated and joyful than I ever imagined! And proud my body had held and given life to such awesomeness!

Decolonizing the spaces of the hospital, the birthing centre, and even the home could serve to transform how women and whānau experience birth. Furthermore, I think we should pursue the possibilities of establishing localized tribally based birthing units. These contemporary birthing houses or units should be grounded in Māori knowledges and tikanga. They can provide a culturally safe space where women and whānau can feel nurtured and supported to birth and mother their babies in a way that upholds and celebrates the uniqueness of Māori maternities. Reinstating the collectivism of maternities and reconfiguring maternity institutions and their practitioners continue to be important parts of decolonization. Also, the government of Aotearoa-New Zealand must recognize these cultural rites and provide for Māori maternities in new and meaningful ways.

Decolonization, also, takes confidence, courage and bravery. Moana Jackson says that we need to be brave, to know who we are, where we have come from, where we are going, and what we need to do to get there: "there are many ways to transform once we identify what we need to transform, and we will each find our own way in which to do it" (76). Linda Smith explains that decolonization is multiple: "it's not just political; the political does not exist out there. It's tied to decolonization of our spirit and about letting our spirit free" (175).

Māori and Indigenous women are involved in a decolonizing politics, whether knowingly or not. Whether through more tectonic forms of resistance or through the more subtle and subversive variety, women and whānau actively negotiate the complexities and intersecting oppressions of colonialism and patriarchy (and often class-based or homophobic oppressions) in their experiences of birth, mothering, and maternities more generally. All of the narratives shared as part of this research highlight that no matter how big or small, every expression of tikanga in birth, afterbirth, and beyond is a powerful act of decolonization and, ultimately, a way of honouring our ancestors, their knowledges and practices, and reclaiming ourselves.

CONCLUSION: HONOURING OUR ANCESTORS, HONOURING OUR FUTURES

This chapter has sought to demonstrate the diverse yet powerful ways that Māori women and whānau are reclaiming Māori knowledges and practices in their pregnancy and birthing experiences in Aotearoa-New Zealand. The silencing of Māori maternities has been resisted and negotiated by generations of women and whanau; the effects, however, are still being felt today. Despite this, the chapter has highlighted the possibilities of reclaiming birth and afterbirth traditions in new and contemporary ways. Honouring our ancestors through the practice of tikanga, such as returning the placenta to the earth, has transformational effects, which extend beyond the individual to the collective, beyond even generations.

The potential for reclaiming Māori maternities is transformative and empowering. The challenge lies in getting to a place where Māori and Indigenous knowledges and practices are not just strands woven into our experiences, but they are the foundations of it. I hope this chapter, in some small way, demonstrates that when we can meet on our own terms and in our own ways, as Māori women and as Māori mothers, the possibilities are endless. Furthermore, transforming the politics of birth can, I believe, also transform the politics of a generation. As such, by honouring our ancestors in pregnancy, birth, and mothering, we honour future generations by providing a "decolonized pathway" (Simpson 28) into, and through, this world for our children and for generations to come.

GLOSSARY

The translations used in this glossary were sourced from *Te Aka: Māori-English, English-Māori Dictionary and Index*. It is important to note that there are multiple meanings and translations available for many of these words. In most cases, I have presented the most common translation(s) of the word or the translation as it is used in the context of this chapter.

Aotearoa – New Zealand
Hapū – subtribe
Ipu whenua – container for the placenta
Iwi – tribe
Karakia – incantation, chant
Kaupapa Māori – Māori-centred theory
Kuia – elderly woman, grandmother
Mana – prestige, authority, control, power, influence
Muka – softened flax fibre
Pākehā – non-Māori New Zealanders
Pounamu – greenstone
Rongoā – remedy, medicine, treatment
Tapu – sacred, set apart, under protection or spiritual deities
Tikanga – procedure, custom, practice, habit
Tūpuna – ancestors
Urupā – burial ground
Waiata – song(s)
Wahine – woman
Wāhine – women
Whakanoa – to make free from the extensions of tapu, ordinary, unrestricted
Whānau – family, to be born, to give birth
Whakapapa – genealogy, descent lines
Whenua – land, placenta

ENDNOTES

[1]Use of the word Māori is in no way meant to homogenize what are in reality diverse knowledges, practices, and experiences; rather, I recognize the tribal and even familial variations and differences. [2]Māori language words will be italicized and translated in brackets on first use and then will be used without italics and translation thereafter. A glossary is provided at the end of the chapter.
[3]Whānau as it is used here refers to wide and diverse conceptualizations of family, and the translation to the English word "family" does not fully encapsulate the multiplicity and extent of the concept of whānau.
[4]Tertiary maternity facilities are designed for women with complex maternity needs that require specialist multidisciplinary care. "Well women" (women who are not deemed to be high risk or have any complicating factors in their pregnancy and labour) may use these facilities in the absence of other maternity facilities in their area. Secondary maternity facilities are designed for women and babies who experience complications and may require care from an obstetrician, an anaesthetist, a paediatrician, or a midwife. Well women may use these facilities in the absence of other maternity facilities in their area. Primary maternity facilities account for 9 percent of all births in New Zealand, and these are made up of maternity units in smaller hospitals and birthing centres. Home births accounted for approximately 3 percent of all births in New Zealand in 2014 (New Zealand, Ministry of Health).
[5]In some instances, food is employed purposefully to whakanoa. For example, at the end of formal ceremonies, such as the pōwhiri (welcome ceremony), visitors are invited to partake in the sharing of food in order to lift the tapu of that ceremony and to enable people to move through that space free of the restrictions of tapu. However, there are other instances where the mixing of food with things or places that are tapu is not seen as culturally appropriate (Pere)—for example the placenta being stored alongside food.

WORKS CITED

Anderson, Kim. "New Life Stirring: Mothering, Transformation and Aboriginal Womanhood." *Until Our Hearts Are on the Ground: Aboriginal Mothering, Oppression, Resistance and Rebirth,* edited by D. Memee Lavell-Harvard and Jeannette Corbiere-Lavell, Demeter Press, 2006, pp. 13-24.

Cram, Fiona, and Linda Tuhiwai Smith. "Māori Women Talk About Accessing Health Care." *He Pukenga Korero: A Journal of Māori Studies,* vol. 7, no. 2, 2003, pp. 1-8.

Cartwright Inquiry. *The Report of the Committee of Inquiry into Allegations Concerning the Treatment of Cervical Cancer at National Women's Hospital and into Other Related Matters.* New Zealand Government Printing Office. 2006.

Donley, Joan. *Birthrites: Natural Vs. Unnatural childbirth in New Zealand,* New Women's Press, 1986.

Gabel, Kirsten. "Poipoia te Tamaiti ki te Ūkaipō." Dissertation, University of Waikato, 2013.

Grace, Patricia. *Cousins.* Penguin 1992.

hooks, bell. *Belonging: A Culture of Place.* Routledge. 1986.

Jackson, Moana. "Hui Reflections: Research and the Consolations of Bravery." *Kei Tua Te Pae Proceedings,* Te Wānanga o Raukawa, New Zealand Council for Education Research, 2011, pp. 71-78.

Kahukiwa, Robyn, and Roma Potiki. *Oriori: A Māori Child Is Born—From Conception to Birth.* Tandem Press. 1999

Kenney, Christine. "Midwives, Women and their Families: A Māori Gaze Regarding Partnerships for Maternity Care in Aotearoa, New Zealand." *AlterNative, Special Issue on Māori Health,* vol. 7, no. 2, 2011, pp. 123-127.

Lavell-Harvard, D. Memee and Jeannette Corbiere-Lavell. *Until Our Hearts Are on the Ground: Aboriginal Mothering, Oppression, Resistance and Rebirth.* Demeter Press, 2006.

Makereti. *The Old-Time Māori.* New Women's Press, 1986.

Mikaere, A. *The Balance Destroyed: Consequences for Māori Women of the Colonisation of Tikanga Māori.* The International Research Institute for Māori and Indigenous Education, 2003.

Mikaere, A. *Colonising Myths-Māori Realities: He Rukuruku Whakaarā.* Huia Publishers and Te Wānanga o Raukawa. 2011.

Moorfield, John C. *Te Aka: Māori-English, English-Māori Dictionary and Index.* Pearson Longman, 2005. Te Whanake.

Murphy, Ngahuia. "Te Awa Atua, Te Awa Tapu, Te Awa Wahine:

An Examination of Stories, Ceremonies and Practices Regarding Menstruation in the Precolonial Māori World." Master's Thesis, University of Waikato, 2011.

New Zealand, Ministry of Health. *Report on Maternity 2014*. Ministry of Health. 2014.

Pere, Rose. *Ako: Concepts and Learning in the Māori Yradition*. Te Kōhanga Reo National Trust Board, 1982.

Simmonds, Naomi. "Tū Te Turuturu Nō Hine-te-iwaiwa: Mana Wahine Geographies of Birth in Aotearoa New Zealand." Dissertation, University of Waikato, 2014.

Simpson, Leanne. "Birthing an Indigenous Resurgence: Decolonizing our Pregnancy and Birthing Ceremonies." *Until Our Hearts Are on the Ground: Aboriginal Mothering, Oppression, Resistance and Rebirth*, edited by D. Memee Lavell-Harvard and Jeannette Corbiere-Lavell, Demeter Press, 2006, pp.25-33.

Smith, Linda Tuhiwai. *Decolonizing Methodologies: Research and Indigenous Peoples*. Zed Books, 2012.

Stevenson, Kendall, et al. "Lived Realities: Birthing Experiences of Maori Women under 20 Years of Age." *AlterNative: An International Journal of Indigenous Peoples*, vol. 12, no. 2, 2016.

7.
Revitalizing Traditional Indigenous Birth Knowledge

REBEKA TABOBONDUNG

TODAY MY SON Zeegwon is ten years old, and I continue to write, research, and engage media arts exploring my experiences of pregnancy, birth, and parenting. Since becoming a mother, my journey has brought me home to Wasauksing First Nation. This is where I began with my thesis research. I spent time listening to Indigenous women's stories to document and share our rich oral histories of traditional birth and working alongside Indigenous midwives, knowledge keepers, storytellers, and health practitioners. During this time, I directed three short films documenting and exploring the journey to revitalize traditional birth knowledge.[1] I believe my ongoing interest speaks to the profound transformative effects becoming a parent can play for individuals and communities. I am compelled to continue to unearth traditional Indigenous birth and parenting knowledge to find innovative ways of sharing it because I believe it holds valuable insights that can contribute to community healing and can find solutions to the power imbalances and intergenerational breakdown of our families and communities brought on by colonization.

REMEMBERING

The first summer after my son Zeegwon was born, my partner and I lived in a small trailer while building our cabin on my home reserve, Wasauksing First Nation. My father, Steven Tabobondung, and many friends camped out with us to help. As I am also a filmmaker, during that summer, I spent time videotaping and talking with my father and my great aunt (Aileen Rice, otherwise known as Aunty-Soda) while my eight-month-old son learned to climb over rocks and tried to gum on fallen acorns. Both my father and Aunty-Soda shared stories with me about my great-grandmother Lucy Tabobondung (Gran) who raised my father and who also was a midwife in our community. My Aunty-Soda told me that her generation was the first to leave the community to have their babies in the hospital in the nearest town, Parry Sound. Before that, midwives like Lucy attended births, which usually took place at home. It was the first time I heard about Gran being a midwife, and the more they spoke of Gran, the more I realized how little I knew of her and our traditional birth knowledge, and a desire to learn more began to grow.

THE DISEMPOWERMENT OF INDIGENOUS WOMEN AND BIRTH KNOWLEDGE

In the last two centuries, processes of colonization have uprooted, silenced, and erased Indigenous birth knowledges and midwifery practices throughout Turtle Island.[2] The Indian Act and the residential school system were major legislated policies, which worked together in an attempt to replace Indigenous culture with the ideologies of the West while containing Indigenous communities and land (Brownlie). With respect to Indigenous birth knowledge, the residential school system also greatly diminished Indigenous oral traditions, which used to ensure the passage of community birth knowledge from one generation to the next (Royal Commission). This legislation affected all aspects of Indigenous people's lives; for Indigenous women, however, not only did they face the inherent racism in these institutions, but they also faced the discrimination of sexism. According to Robin Jarvis Brownlie, federal policy was designed "to impose a European patriarchal model of gender relations on Aboriginal people, enforcing female dependence on men" (163).[3] Wasauksing women also experienced this discrimination, which Brownlie describes below:

> One such woman was Julia K., who lived on Parry Island Reserve.... She suffered from rheumatism, all her children

130

had tuberculosis, and the family had been abandoned by her husband.... Mrs. K was known to the agents for her outspokenness (Daly [the Indian Agent] remarked, "This woman has a tongue"), and thus she was a thorn in their sides. In 1933 Indian agent H.J. Eade wrote to Daly about Mrs. K's agitation for improved relief issues. Eade insisted that she was "getting more than her share"... He added, "Further I hear she is doing some running around with other men." He advised Daly to "watch her very closely," and if she were involved in sexual relationships, to cut off her relief. (166)

Indian Agents enforced the Indian Act in our communities, and these civil servants of the state wielded extraordinary powers over Indigenous communities (Brownlie, 160). Since the Indian Act had stripped women of their access to resources, women were more likely than men to be in positions of financial need, which led to closer surveillance and control over their lives (Brownlie 161). The regulation of First Nations women focused particularly on gender and sexual behaviour. The ideals of passivity and submission of Western gendered roles extended into the arena of childbirth and medicine, and Indigenous women were made to feel their way of life and the knowledges associated with it were primitive and of little worth. As Sapna Patel and Iman Al-Jazairi explain, "The early imperialists initiated the demonization of the traditional lay midwife. By portraying her as superstitious, barbarous, and repulsive, they formed a stereotype based on falsified information" (60).

According to Myra Rutherdale, nurse missionaries—such as Sarah Stringer stationed at Fort Selkirk, Yukon in the late 1930s—hoped that in return for successful Western medical care, First Nations women would be convinced to "give up their evil and superstitious ways" and abandon traditional medicine (233). Rutherdale provides a narrative of an Aivilingmiut birthing experience described by settler Reverend Donald Marsh as a "turning point," in which he claimed "the cruel ways of the past began to change for the good of the people" (qtd. in Rutherdale 233).

Inside were Caroline [a Christian Aivilingmiut who was

about to give birth] and her mother-in-law [also a Christian Aivilingmiut], all the camp midwives and angakoks [traditional Elders]. Win [Marsh's White wife] stopped, looked around, and asked Caroline, "Do you want to have your baby this way" The answer was a quick "No!" Win politely asked the angakoks and midwives to leave and then rolled down the tent flaps, restoring privacy. (Marsh qtd. in Rutherdale 233)

The devaluing of Indigenous birth knowledge caused many daughters to no longer value the traditional knowledge of their mothers because they viewed it as superstitious and primitive, which broke the passing down of family and cultural knowledges. For example, an Anishinaabe woman describes this rupture within her own family:

[This knowledge] ... goes back to our great-grandmother. I wanted to teach it to my daughter when she was here last week, but she wouldn't even listen to me; she said she didn't believe any of it. None of my children believe in the old Indian ways; maybe they will when they grow older and wiser. Since no one but my sister and I have this knowledge, and we won't live much longer, it will die when we go; it belongs only to our family. (qtd. in Hilger 11)

According to a National Aboriginal Health Organization report titled: *Midwifery and Aboriginal Midwifery in Canada*, "many ancient birth and midwifery practices have been lost [systematically eliminated] and few Aboriginal midwives are left to pass along Indigenous knowledge in this and other areas" (NAHO 7). Western birth practices and values are now forced on Indigenous women and have become normalized. Colonization and colonial education have fragmented our oral traditions by attempting to sever our capacity as communities to transmit knowledge to our children.

THE REVITALIZATION OF TRADITIONAL BIRTH KNOWLEDGE

As Indigenous people, we have the strength of our culture and ancestors to thank for our continued survival. The information included, while centred on personal experiences, is also based on community-grounded traditional knowledge. Traditional Indigenous knowledge, including birth knowledge, is founded within the oral traditions of our ancestors. To revitalize our understanding of and connection to traditional birth knowledges, we must spend time recalling our pre-contact knowledges. Although the research looks to reclaim and rejuvenate ancestral knowledge based on the oral tradition, it also includes contemporary stories that when taken together demonstrate the resilience of our traditions against powerful assimilationist policies; these stories also acknowledge, though, that our realities as individuals and communities have shifted as a result of these influences.

A RICH AND HIGHLY DEVELOPED BIRTHING CULTURE

As part of my research, I spent time with three Wasauksing community members who represent three generations of experience as mothers, and I asked them to share their experience and understanding of traditional birth knowledge. To my great honour, the following women agreed to participate: Marie Anderson (Elder and great-grandmother), Faith Pegahmagabow (mid-life and grandmother), and Harmony Rice (youth and new mother). The women shared personal and traditional stories painting a picture of a highly communal and spiritual society in which pregnancy, childbirth, and the newborn are considered sacred and honoured as central to the community and to communication. Prior to contact, Anishinabek communities had a rich and highly developed birthing culture, which included a whole community approach to care and responsibility for ensuring the wellbeing of the expecting family. The following represents a small excerpt of the immense knowledge these women shared with me.

TEACHINGS AND INSIGHT

She was to take care of herself in a good way and be of good mind of good heart, of good body, so that the community and family, they had a responsibility to her to make sure that she didn't have to worry about things. [She] didn't have to worry about where her next meal would come from, or if she was going to have enough food, if she was going to have a good shelter, if she was going to be warm; they needed to take care of her so she wouldn't have to worry about opening herself up to negative things. (Faith Pegahmagabow)

The interviewed women reiterated the values of balance in all aspects of life and relationships. This balance included the relationship between humans and the natural world; between community members; between men and women; and between the spiritual, emotional, intellectual, and physical parts of the self. The women spoke about the importance of pregnant mothers maintaining inner balance and how it promotes healthy pregnancies, births, and children. This teaching extends to the father and to the community, because this inner balance cannot be achieved if an expectant mother must also secure the family's livelihood. She must rely on the community for support. Thus, for Wasauksing, the community is also the centre of life.

MAINTAIN BALANCE AND CALM

Sometimes when children are small, very small, you'll hear them at night wake up in a scream. It's not a bad dream; they're seeing something, what his mother or father did before he was born. They're going through that because that child was there inside the mother. (Marie Anderson)

Women are responsible for ensuring a healthy pregnancy, labour, and newborn by maintaining balance between the emotional and physical aspects of themselves, through exercise, nutrition, and avoiding stressful situations. They share the responsibility of maintaining the spiritual wellbeing of their unborn children with the fathers and the general community. Faith explained that a pregnant woman is responsible "for being in a good frame of mind," because a baby in utero can be affected and influenced by its parent's emotions and experiences. Such a vital understanding contributes to the development of a healthy baby, but if not maintained, it can lead to repercussions affecting the baby throughout his or her life.

Faith remarked that a pregnant woman had to be conscious of her actions and reactions "because those characteristics or emotions affect how that baby develops." For example, Faith indicated if the woman "was angry a lot in her pregnancy, she's going to have an angry baby. So you couldn't be nasty to somebody because you know that was going to affect how your child developed." Marie shared that the teachings of maintaining balance and calm were also imparted to her: "The biggest teaching I heard was if something happens over there, like if somebody falls or takes a seizure, don't go there because that baby's going to adopt that." Marie commented that a pregnant woman "must not let anything startle her, like if she's walking through the bush she might run across a snake that would startle her and when she gives birth to her baby, the baby will have that reaction."

THE FATHER IS ALSO PREGNANT

Each participant discussed the important role that the father plays in the pregnancy for ensuring the baby's healthy development. The value of balance is extended to the father, who like the mother, is viewed as pregnant and must also achieve inner and spiritual balance. He is also responsible for maintaining his physical health, which includes achieving an inner and outer balance and calm, and for respecting all life. Marie explained that a pregnant man "could not participate in any hunting; he could not participate in any fishing." Men had to refrain from participating in activity involving death or suffering to ensure the child's healthy development: "if they were out hunting and fishing or trapping, they couldn't go over there and handle those animals; somebody else has to go because it all depends how that animal suffered before he died." Faith also explained that when a woman "was carrying that new life, he [the father] couldn't be taking life, so he couldn't hunt or fish." She explained that "his clan family[4] and the community came to support them by doing his hunting and his fishing. So they took care of that family's needs so that man could honour life by not taking life." The father was thus able to maintain his role, to contribute "to nurture that new life that's coming."

The massive restrictions placed on the pregnant parents such as not being permitted to hunt or handle dead animals made them entirely dependent on their families and the community for their most basic needs. In other words, the community is entirely responsible for this new family's wellbeing. Although traditional birth knowledge, such as the role of the midwife, is beginning to once again be embraced in our communities, Harmony pointed out that the integral role men once played in maintaining healthy pregnancies needs to be revived. "Some men in our community, even if they're having a kid, they're just the same guy that they always are. Whereas in history, our teaching was when the woman is pregnant, there are all these things that the man doesn't do, refrains from doing, or does more of." Faith also reiterated something similar: "The Nishnaabe people always said when a woman is pregnant so is the man; he's pregnant too. This was our teaching."

Men being pregnant is a concept that cannot be contained within Western defined gender roles and shows, as Faith explains, that men and women "both have responsibilities" in making healthy lifestyle choices affecting the wellbeing of their child. When speaking on the topic of health, Harmony spoke of drugs and alcohol, and explained that "pregnant women in our history weren't to go near any other bad spirits, which includes drugs and alcohol because they could have a negative influence."[5] Faith added that men were also forbidden to abuse drugs or alcohol, which could negatively affect one's spirit including that of the unborn child "because when that father leaves and goes where ever, say he's going to the bar, that little one's spirit goes with him too because that's their father, that's the dad so they go with him." Harmony recalled the positive experience she felt when she and her partner became pregnant, they "stopped any sort of negative lifestyle choices that we may have had before. He totally stopped with me and that was such an honour to our child that he did that."

Faith indicated that "the father is supposed to be talking to that baby in utero." To communicate love and cultural knowledge, he talks "about its clan family about the clan songs, talking to it in the language, telling it about what its life is going to be like when it gets here and how much its loved and how much it's wanted." According to Faith, the "child is learning right from conception and that child hears everything that is going on outside and so that's why you treat it and its mother in a good way." Faith elaborated that the father's responsibility is to "treat the mother in a good way, and she looks after herself too, but she shouldn't have any worries." Harmony shared this view and reiterated that fathers "would help the woman in preparing for the baby, so if it meant going out to pick berries for the feast for the baby when the baby gets its name or going to help the woman to pick cedar, the man would do that with her."

Maintaining balance is integral to an Anishinabek worldview. It is logical that men are also considered pregnant because men too must contribute, grow, and learn in preparation for becoming fathers and raising healthy children.

COMMUNITY RESPONSIBILITIES

The pregnant parents' family and the community not only ensured the physical safety of the mother but also provided for their basic needs. The restrictions placed on expecting parents made them dependent on the community. The women talked about the essential role of the community in taking care of the pregnant couple. According to Marie, "As soon as a girl was pregnant the word was passed around so everybody could be there for this woman." Marie explained that the community ensures the safety and wellbeing of the mother by not leaving her unattended and warning her of potential danger. "It's just like walking into glass. If you know somebody's headed that way where the pile of glass is, you're not going to let them walk over there because they're going to hurt themselves. This was the same teaching they had." Marie elaborated that "pregnancy is very sacred and they always said because of that, somebody must be with this woman all the time. It could either be her man or a friend or a sister or a brother or an in-law." The community takes care of the most basic needs of the pregnant mother and father ensuring a healthy, stress free pregnancy for the mother and the spiritual protection of the child through the love and communication of both contributing parents.

Members of the community also have the responsibility of sharing their knowledge with the couple. Harmony explained that there are "women in the community that will do specific things for pregnant women, like they will come to see you, they'll come to visit you, they'll come to give you things, to pass knowledge on." Marie elaborated, "each person had a different responsibility for that woman." For example, if someone knew the pregnant woman was not a good cook, "she'd take blueberries and some flour and she'd go and show her how to make blueberry pie." Harmony listed specific things that certain individuals would do for babies born in the community of Wasauksing:

> One woman will make a traditional quilt with a medicine wheel here in our community for babies and there's another woman who'll knit their first outfit that they go home in with their booties and their hat and their sweater. There are other women that will go and pick the cedar for that cedar bath that the baby has. There's other women that tell pregnant women what to do with their pregnancy how they should be eating how they shouldn't be eating.

Marie, Harmony, and Faith explained that expecting parents should learn about community relationships and understand their family and clan relationships to ensure choosing an appropriate partner and to transmit this knowledge to their child. Harmony explained that "In our community now and in history there is responsibility placed on pregnant women [and men]" to listen and learn when "people come to talk to you about how you're going to raise your baby." Harmony said that the purpose of these conversations is to ensure "you have your name"[6] and find out "if you know what your clan is, if you know what your partner's clan is, what community they come from." Harmony recalled that when she was pregnant "all of sudden everybody wanted to know who my partner was, and wanted to know what his traditional connection was, and were we related through our clans." She pointed out that "just having those conversations really impacted my whole perception of how we regard relationships." She had the responsibility of knowing the "A, B, C and D about who I was and about who my partner was and how we were going to do it." Harmony recalled that as a result of the pregnancy and listening to community members, her partner "went out to go and get his clan; he started to ask around about his spirit name, started to do research about his family history so that he would know where he came from and who he was, and what communities he had ties to." Harmony described the process of listening and learning about her and her partner's relationship and identities within the community as a very positive experience that contributed in preparing for her role as a mother: "I remember it was probably one of the times in my life where I felt most loved. I felt like we were doing all the right things in a good way in terms of laying the foundation for our daughter to come into the world."

Marie, Faith, and Harmony described preparing for a baby in terms not based on material wealth or consumerism but on maintaining calm, balance, and centring community. Marie and Faith both shared their concerns with mainstream baby showers commonly held prior to the birth of a child in the community today. Marie shared that at a baby shower the "baby is overloaded with gifts before he arrives," and according to the Elders, "he can't handle that; it's like a shock. That's why they say to wait last minute." Faith reiterated this point: "My mother always told me that we don't have baby showers until after the baby comes. How I see that fitting in with our traditional practices is, that's part of the welcoming and that's when we bring the gifts for the child. So it's not just a women thing; it's a community event."

CONCLUSION

The knowledge shared by Marie, Faith and Harmony attests to a community that values community and traditional birth knowledge by refusing to forget our most sacred relationships. It also attests to the magnitude of intact birth knowledge that exists and continues to be practiced in Wasauksing today. Based on patriarchal beliefs, the Indian Act stripped our natural right to mother our children and transmit our culture, which values balance and the sacredness in all Creation and life, especially female life because of our own life-giving capabilities (Anderson; Pegahmagabow). At the same time, Indigenous men were given exclusive control over lands and community leadership which led to the double discrimination of women and further deteriorated balance in our communities so highly sought and valued prior to contact.

However with Indigenous traditions, men have important roles to contribute that foster balance, responsibility, and sharing. Faith discussed how "men are also responsible for the creation of new life and therefore must also be taught to honour it and understand their important role as men and fathers and providers for their families and community." This perspective of valuing all life is also important because it rejects oppressive hierarchies, which value one life over another (Anderson). The women discussed the many gendered roles and responsibilities that community members maintained. Here I am reminded of the equality movement within feminist thinking which seeks "equality" between genders in an effort to eliminate women's oppression by affording women equal rights and power as men. Like the author Kim Anderson, I have wondered if the gender roles in Wasauksing, described by the women I interviewed, are oppressive in the same ways they are in Western society. Following Anderson, I also conclude it defies comparison, as it is rooted in an Indigenous worldview in which balance is integral within gendered relationships and the roles and responsibilities placed on both are recognized as interdependent and, thus, both valued (Anderson 213). This is especially true for new parents in Wasauksing, where according to Marie Anderson, fathers slept on a hard floor to empathize with the challenges of sleep deprivation from breastfeeding a newborn, which compelled him to help as much as possible.

Recalling our birth knowledges honours our identities and traditions. Since new life and community are integral to these traditions, it also honours our children, strengthens community building, and mends the negative effects of colonization. Although the research acknowledges that our realities as individuals and communities have been shifted as a result of powerful assimilationist policies and influences, it also looks to reclaim and rejuvenate ancestral knowledge based on the oral tradition. These contemporary stories experienced by multiple generations of Wasauksing women demonstrate the continued resilience of our birth traditions.

ENDNOTES

[1] *Wasauksing Women Sharing Strength*, 2008; *For Seven Generations: Visioning an Aboriginal Birth Centre in Toronto*, 2012; and *Spirit of Birth*, 2015.

[2] The name Turtle Island refers to the land base also known today as North America. It is translated from numerous Indigenous creation stories and languages, and its use reinforces the concept of title to the land.

[3] The Indian Act not only governs the life of 350,000 Native Indians in Canada, it also defines who is and is not legally an "Indian." From 1869 until 1985, the determination of Indian status was determined by a patrilineal system; that is, by a person's relationship to "a male person who is a direct descendent in the male line of a male person." When a status woman married a non-status man, she lost her status, and could not regain it, even if she subsequently was divorced or widowed. Along with her status, the woman lost her band membership and with it, her property, inheritance, residency, burial, medical, educational, and voting rights on the reserve. In direct contrast, an Indian man bestowed his status upon his wife and their children. Consequently, every Indian woman was dependent upon a man—first her father and then her husband—for her identity, rights, and status under the Indian Act (qtd. in Silman 12).

[4] The Anishinabek follow a clan system based on kinship relations or "super families," which along with other spiritual beliefs, aided them in securing order and friendship in and between communities (Clifton et al. 77). The clans are based on animals, and members of the same clan were regarded as brother and sister and could not marry. "In almost every village that existed in the historical past, a member of a particular clan was able to find a relative: a brother or a sister of the same clan. This extended kinship system ... provided an atmosphere of security and well-being, since no matter where the Anishnaabeg went, they had relatives who were obligated to provide assistance because of common identity" (77). Faith explained that in the Ojibway tradition, the children follow the father's clan.

[5] It is a common belief in Indigenous communities that alcohol

negatively affects one's spirit.

[6]Harmony is referring to a traditional or spirit name that is usually revealed and presented by an Elder based on their personal communication with the spirit world. A traditional name is essentially one's name in the spirit world, which identifies and describes one's spirit, and when bestowed and heeded upon, it can act to protect and be a guide throughout one's life.

WORKS CITED

Anderson, Kim. *A Recognition of Being Reconstructing Native Womanhood.* Sumach Press. 2000.

Anderson, Marie. Personal interview. July. 2007.

Brownlie, Jarvis, Robin. "Intimate Surveillance: Indian Affairs, Colonization, and the Regulation of Aboriginal Women's Sexuality." *Contact Zones: Aboriginal & Settler Women in Canada's Colonial Past,* edited by Katie Pickles and Myra Rutherdale, University of British Columbia Press, 2005, pp. 160-78.

Clifton, James, et al. *People of The Three Fires: The Ottawa, Potawatomi and Ojibway Of Michigan.* The Michigan Indian Press Grand Rapids Inter-Tribal Council, 1986.

Hilger, Inez. *Chippewa Child Life and Its Cultural Background.* 1951. Minnesota Historical Society Press, 1992.

National Aboriginal Health Organization. *Midwifery and Aboriginal Midwifery in Canada,* National Aboriginal Health Organization. 2004, www.naho.ca/documents/naho/english/publications/DP_aboriginal_midwifery.pdf. Accessed 30 Aug. 20167.

Patel, Sapna, and Iman Al-Jazairi. "Colonized Wombs." *The New Midwifery: Rejections on Renaissance and Regulation,* edited by Farah M. Shroff, Women's Press, 1997, pp. 51-82.

Pegahmagabow, Faith. Personal interview. July. 2007.

Rice, Harmony. Personal interview. August. 2007.

Royal Commission on Aboriginal Peoples. *Report of the Royal Commission on Aboriginal Peoples.* Volumes 1-5. Government of Canada, 1996.

Rutherdale, Myra. "'She was a Ragged Little Thing': Missionaries, Embodiment, and Refashioning Aboriginal Womanhood in Northern Canada." *Contact Zones: Aboriginal & Settler*

Women in Canada's Colonial Past, edited by Katie Pickles and Myra Rutherdale, University of British Columbia Press, 2005, pp. 228-45.

Silman, Janet. *Enough is Enough Aboriginal Women Speak Out.* The Women's Press. 1987.

8.
Birth Places, Embodied Spaces

Tlicho Pregnancy Stories across the Generations

LESLIE DAWSON

T HE FORCED CULTURE CHANGES of colonization in Canada
affected Indigenous societies at different points in time; colonization of the Tlicho (formerly Dogrib) region in the Northwest
Territories (NWT) was considered to have been relatively recent.
The profound changes to the lives of the Tlicho can be heard in the
stories across the generations. To investigate the impact of colonization on Tlicho maternal health, I collected pregnancy and the birth
stories from Tlicho women of different generations.[1] Generations
were further expanded with the addition of Joan Ryan's work with
Tlicho Elders in Whati, NWT, and Pertice Moffitt's discussions
with younger Tlicho women in Behchoko, NWT. I collected pregnancy and birth stories from ten Tlicho women between the ages
of sixty through ninety in the Tlicho communities of Behchoko
and Whati over the summers of 2013 and 2014. The women met
with me in their homes and most shared their stories in Tlicho
with the aid of an interpreter. Grounded in women's narratives,
particularly of Tlicho Elders and a traditional midwife, their stories
reveal changes in the lived experiences of pregnancy and birth as
reflecting different sociohistoric locations within histories of colonization—from birth on the land with community and midwives,
to the beginnings of settlement and birth in the mission hospital in
Rae, and to lone evacuation to Yellowknife for medicalized birth
in a biomedical hospital.

Birth, however, is not solely a physiological event but is shaped
by cultural values and meanings, nor is a birth place simply a location in which a physiological event occurs. Since places are not

only "in the landscape but simultaneously in the land, people's minds, customs, and bodily practices" (Munn qtd. in Low 15), birth places may be seen as social and cultural spaces endowed with cultural values and meanings fundamental in the rituals of birth. Similarly, the body may be seen as both biological and social and cultural. Through the intersection of space, place, and the body, a space becomes embodied or, as Low describes, an "embodied space," in which meaning is inscribed on the body (10-11). By considering changing Tlicho birth places as embodied spaces, I explore the social transformations in time and space brought about by the processes of missionization and medicalization to reveal how colonial histories of controlling birth experiences have become inscribed on Tlicho maternal bodies.

BIRTH ON THE LAND: THE FEMALE BODY AS POWERFUL

The Tlicho are a Dene people occupying the region between Great Slave Lake and Great Bear Lake in the Northwest Territories. Today the Tlicho live in the four communities of Behchoko, Whati, Gameti, and Wekweeti. However, the traditional setting for the Tlicho saw extended families living on the land in bush camps for most of the year—hunting, trapping, and fishing seasonally. Women gave birth in the bush camps with the assistance of other women, including midwives. When a woman was "sick" (in labour), a pole was placed sideways for the woman to hold onto. She would kneel or position herself in a sitting or squat position with someone holding onto her. The midwife, or other women assisting in the birth, would rub her stomach to help reduce the pain and to help the baby to be delivered faster. Once the baby was born, a midwife would tie and cut the umbilical cord, and apply a variety of medicines from the land, including rotten wood, black coal, or burnt dry willow, to help the cord heal and prevent infection. After cleaning the baby, the afterbirth was delivered. The mother was then cleaned up, and the baby was encouraged to breastfeed. The mother was then expected to rest for about a week, with other women assisting her, until she healed. Tlicho women, including Elders, recounted their childhood memories of birth on the land:

Dene woman with baby in a moss carrier Fort Rae, 1924.
NWT Archives/Canada. Dept. of the Interior fonds./G-1979-001: 0165

I saw twice but an Elder they chase us out. By the time we came back the woman was holding the baby ... First I hear a baby cry.... I remember that it was me and my cousin, we're just sleeping, all suddenly whole bunch of women coming in and wood stove going fire ... hurry up, hurry up.... I was wondering how come they are all rushing just banging, stove going, fire going, washing water's boiling, so there must have been about four or five midwives there helping each other and if anything goes wrong they know how to, how to [turn the baby]. That's why they were all there you know. Instructing each other like help each other. (TPS003)

Although some Elders recalled tragic birth events in which a woman died during delivery, they told other stories with laughter as they recalled being chased away by Elders: "As little kids, we peek in the little hole in the tent, we peek in there and they say, you guys don't look.... Because of you guys the baby's hard to be born.... It's so funny looking through" (TPS008).

As James Waldram and colleagues (145-6) note, a widespread belief maintains that healing roles in Indigenous societies were primarily held by males (e.g., medicine men), and this may reflect a gender bias in the historical record, as European males would have been excluded from observing female activities or from speaking with them. Indigenous women did occupy healing roles, despite the poor state of the literature. Almost no details on Indigenous childbirth practices exist (147). Indeed, women were highly skilled birth attendants employing a variety of surgical practices and medicines from the land.

Tlicho midwives were "gifted" and attended to not only births but "sicknesses" as well:

Women whose hands are really gentle that the woman doesn't feel the pain, but still some women who are touching the woman experiencing giving birth they're just in so much pain. "There are some people with different gifts," that's what [my mother-in-law] said. That's the reason she was always being called. It's just like whenever a woman is giving birth. Not only that, other kind of sickness too, she was being called. (TPS001)

A traditional Tlicho midwife explained how her own mother, also a midwife, directed her to become a midwife:

> Because [I] had seen so many babies delivered that that's the reason why [my] mom gave [me] the message that, after I'm passed you will help woman's delivery of babies cause you've seen so much and you've seen lots and you know how to do it and you know how they feel, so every woman that's sick with pregnancy [I] come over when her time is near for the delivery of the baby. (TPS005)

Other stories related women's knowledge of a variety of medicines from the land; indeed, in discussions with Elders in Whati, Ryan recorded a variety of spiritual approaches and traditional medicines—including spruce boughs, Labrador tea, tamarack, and otters chin—for a variety of concerns, such as engorged breasts, problems conceiving, breech births, and retained placentas (*Traditional Dene Medicine, Part II*, 227-51). As one Tlicho Elder recalled, "After the delivery they boil that kind [of spruce bough] and they let the woman drink the juice, you know, to heal fast and not to feel pain any more cause after delivery they have pain, you know inside their tummy. So they let them drink that kind and then they don't feel pain. They heal fast" (TPS008).

A traditional midwife shared the story of delivering her daughter's baby, which needed to be repositioned:

> [My] daughter was in labour. What happened was the baby was coming out but one side of the arm came out instead, you know the baby was sideway.... What [I] did then was put a lot of soap, lard on [my] hands and asked daughter if she's awake or you know conscious. She said yes so [I] pushed the baby back in and turned the baby around. But that was the way to deliver breech, the baby standing up. And that's how [I] delivered the baby, feet first. (TPS005)

Dene woman with child on her back, Fort Rae, [n.d.].
NWT Archives/Henry Busse fonds/N-1979-052: 1727

Knowledge of wellbeing during pregnancy and birth was passed from Elders, grandmothers, and mothers to daughters: "Wherever they are, wherever the people, women are, you know, they just deliver the baby. Even the mothers they learn it from their mothers. I think that's how it was" (TPS008). By observing, experiencing, storytelling, and teaching, ways of knowing how to be well were passed on:

> The elderly women, their mothers, they always encourage their daughters and they encourage their grandchild, granddaughter.... They carry a child so be careful. Don't eat that kind, they would tell you that ... they were very watchful. But in those days the women were really strong, they were tough. (TPS001)

Another Tlicho woman recalled specific advice:

> They used to tell them.... they have to move around so
> that their delivery, if the labour comes, it will be easier for
> them to deliver the baby. They had to move around all the
> time...so the baby can move around inside their womb.
> They used to tell them that if they don't move around too
> much then the baby will ... attach to the womb and it will
> be hard for the baby to come out.... It's gonna be stuck.
> (TPS008)

However, birth on the land involved more than the delivery of a
child and the wellbeing of the mother. For the Tlicho, life on the
land reflected the interconnected nature of humans, animals, and
spirituality. Humans had reciprocal and responsible relationships
with animals and the land. All living things had a life force, as
reflected in the rituals of the hunt and the respect for the animals
shown through these rituals. For instance, when a moose was
killed, the bell was hung in a tree so other game would know that
it had been handled properly and taken with thanks. Moose would
then return to that area to be taken again (Ryan, *Traditional Dene
Justice* 24). Similarly, after a kill and butchering, no parts could be
left on the ground, and bones had to be covered by rocks or put
in trees so the moose or caribou might reclaim them for its next
life. If these rules were not followed, the animal would be offended
and would not return to the area. Blood was handled carefully,
since it represented the animal's life force (Ryan, *Traditional Dene
Justice* 24-5). Furthermore, mistreatment of bones could lead to
sickness and/or bad luck for the hunter as one Tlicho Elder shared:

> They don't throw bones anywhere because people don't
> go over it ... if its elsewhere and the people go over it, you
> know, walk over it or something, they can get sick with
> it ... they live on traditional food off the land and if they
> don't respect their bones, they just throw them somewhere
> that's how you're not lucky, even to go on the land, you
> know, food ... bad luck with the hunter. You have to have
> respect for it. (TPS006)

As with the invisibility of women in the literature in terms of Indigenous healing roles, most research has focused on the reciprocal relationship of the male hunter and the animals, and not about the responsibilities of females. However, everyone had responsibilities toward the hunt, including women. Beyond the practical aspects of preparing men for the hunt (e.g., clothing, food), woman also had a responsibility to maintain the balance between humans, animals, and the spirit world. In particular, women's blood (i.e., menstrual blood and the blood associated with childbirth) was seen as powerful; therefore, a variety of disciplined female behaviours were expected so as to not endanger the hunt: "A woman's blood could draw strength away from the hunter" (Ryan, *Traditional Dene Justice* 23). Although the concept of "contamination" of trails and gear by women's blood is popular in the ethnographic literature on hunting-trapping societies, as Ryan clarifies, the Elders challenged this term. Instead, the term "endanger" rather than contamination was proposed, as it highlighted women's power and her ability to draw power away from men, which would affect their ability to hunt and endanger the group's survival:

> Women could not step over meat, blood of hunting gear, menstruating women could not handle blood, and pubescent girls could not handle meat or blood, as women's blood could draw strength away from a hunter, even if he was on the trail and she was in camp. Animals also knew when a woman stepped over game or gear and would be affected enough to not allow themselves to be taken. (Ryan, *Traditional Dene Justice* 24)

Upon puberty, Tlicho girls learned how to control their power and followed a variety of rituals. Pubertal girls were isolated in menstrual teepees, where they collected their own wood, water, and sometimes food. The experience was said to make them strong and to connect them to the spirit world (Ryan, *Traditional Dene Justice* 39). Girls (as well as boys) were also "tied" by their grandmothers; moose straps were tied to their ankles, waist, wrist, and neck. This was done to give them strength, courage, and wisdom, and also protected them from evil spirits (40). As one Tlicho woman recalled:

> After, you know, when they get their first period they have to tie their fingers together with hide. They tie it together; it's always like this. So you know there's not gap in between the fingers. As they grow up, they will always have their fingers like that until their monthly goes…. They have to keep it tied until the monthly goes away and then you know they undo it, and when their monthly comes again they do it like every month. (TPS008)

The desire to balance the relationship between animals, humans, and the spiritual world, as evidenced in the rituals of the hunt, was also mirrored in birth rituals. Because of the male role in hunting, "the husband does not sleep with his wife for a month [following the birth of a child]. She will sleep by herself with the child" (TPS001). Following birth, the mother's movements were restricted because of her power:

> As soon as the baby is born, they don't walk around inside they stay where they are; if they are going out they have to pull up the side of the tent and go out from there, they don't go out the doorway. They go out from the women's side of the tent to avoid sickness. Women would have their own cup and they would tie a string or something around the cup or the handle. That lady who has the baby can't use anybody's cup. This would last until she stops bleeding [either menstruation or the bleeding associated with child-birth]. They would also have their own washroom [similar to the menstrual teepees], separate from the men's. (TPS008)

Another woman explained the interrelationships of people and animals in the traditional treatment of the umbilical cord and afterbirth:

> You cut the cord when the baby you know the cord comes out… Sometimes they cut the trees or the wood… [she] says

you put it [umbilical cord] up there and then hop around, dance around, you know ... give you luck to this child. Either they dance around or they just talk to it. And so they say when the whiskey jack comes and when it picks up the baby's cord they say this whiskey jack is going to be directing this guy for a good hunt ... I always questioned [my mother-in-law] ... you know when a baby is born, the afterbirth when it comes out, I said what do you do with those things you know because I remember when I worked in the hospital you know they just threw it away ... [She] said sometimes if this child has been gifted, what they do is they bury that thing, they bury it, either on top of the tree or they bury it on top the ... you know, pole rack up there.... Yeah, eagle or some kind of animals ... you know, bear or type of animal ... you know, they say it takes it and that's how the child would grew well healthy and strong, you know, until he grows until manhood. Just like they would have prediction. (TPS001)

Birth on the land, therefore, reflected the interconnected nature of humans, animals, and spirituality. The relationship to the land informed the rituals of birth and emplaced Tlicho birth experiences. However, these rituals of birth would be suppressed as Tlicho spirituality came under the missionaries' agenda of assimilation. As Waldram and his colleagues discuss, Indigenous medical systems were subjected to a variety of oppressive measures; measures not aimed at medical practices per se but rather at aspects of Indigenous spiritualties and social life deemed to be prohibitive of assimilation (147). With suppression of Tlicho spirituality came a new interpretation of the female body.

MISSIONIZED BIRTH: THE FEMALE BODY AS SUFFERING

Missionization in the North, as with other areas of Indigenous Canada, began with a desire to save Indigenous "souls" through conversion to Christianity. As Waldram and colleagues explain, this dominant theme influenced other forms of forced assimilation couched in humanitarian, Christian terms. Since Indigenous people lacked knowledge of God, Jesus, and the sacraments, they were seen as "savages" in need of paternalistic care to become "civilized" (i.e., assimilated into Euro-Canadian cultural patterns and belief systems) (14). More Catholic institutions were eventually established, including residential schools, which removed the children from their oral traditions and the continuity of their generations.

The first missionaries arrived in the Fort Rae area around 1852, and with the missionaries came epidemics of infectious diseases. The traditional Dene belief systems could not account for, or counteract, the disastrous new epidemics that decimated communities. The loss of significant numbers of community members altered leadership roles and disrupted existing social structures, and paved the way for the onslaught by European Christian missionaries (Waldram et al. 291).

Although the first doctor came to the region in 1900, visiting annually, infectious diseases (measles, tuberculosis, and influenza) took their toll in the 1920s and 1930s (Ryan, *Traditional Dene Justice* 113), and the Faraud Mission Hospital was established in Fort Rae (Behchoko) in 1940. As part of the Roman Catholic Mission, the hospital setting revealed a shift in the transfer of women's knowledge of birth:

> At the hospital, the nuns delivered the babies without a doctor. The nuns would gather all the pregnant women and would teach them on how they're going to deliver the baby. That's how the nuns there explain it to them. Just like teaching so they know. Once we know, once they deliver the baby and everything was good, they took good care of you and everything was okay. (TPS008)

Despite the establishment of the mission hospital, people continued to live and give birth on the land until the development of the communities of Whati, Gameti, and Wekweeti in the 1960s and 1970s. In some cases, some women simply did not want to go to the hospital and wanted a midwife: "She was going to have a baby so they told her to go. Well, there was an old hospital here [Fort Rae] with nuns, sisters, but no doctor. So they asked her to go to

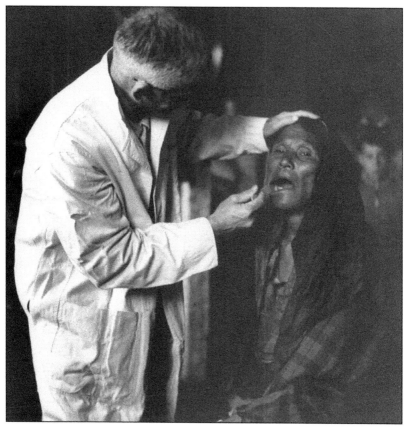

Dr. J.H. Riopel, District Medical Officer and Indian Agent, examines a Dogrib patient at Fort Rae, 1939. NWT Archives/Richard Finnie fonds/N-1979-063: 0053

the hospital but she wouldn't listen. She doesn't want to have the baby deliver there" (TPS005).

As Ryan notes, the overlay between Dene belief systems and Christian ones was extensive in the initial contact period; both became entwined and included many similar interpretations of the world and its Creator and spiritual events. This overlay of interpretations seems evident in stories related by the Elders. In discussions with the Elders about women's role in surgery (i.e., Caesarean sections), Ryan describes how the group had, at first, agreed that a baby would not be removed through Caesarean if the woman had died during pregnancy, but then a story was recounted:

[A woman] was sick or injured during the pregnancy and

died. They didn't know what to do with her; they couldn't leave the body like that. The relatives asked Monique [a midwife] for help. Monique felt miserable having to make a decision about what to do. She told the other women not to mourn because she would take care of things. They prepared the body for surgery. While sharping the knife, she thought of the Creator. It would not be right to have the child buried inside the mother. She knew the Creator would give her the courage to perform the surgery and to do his will. She cut the stomach open. She wasn't afraid nor did she feel terrible. The body was partially frozen. She wasn't sure how far to cut down from the ribs so she cut across the abdomen. Then she took the baby out, placed it on a canvas cloth. Then she sewed the mother back up. Monique told this story to Marie Madeline Nitsiza. Not any one could do this type of surgery. It takes someone with a strong mind like herself who has spiritual powers. She was smart to use her spiritual power. She was a powerful spiritual person. They place the child under the mother's arm for burial. (*Traditional Dene Medicine, Part II*, 230)

Monique's daughter, also a midwife, recounted this story. After describing her admiration for her mother's strength, she stated clearly that she wanted the nurses or anyone else to know that if a woman dies with a baby in the womb, it must be taken out and that she wanted the story to go on. As she said, "this is why I give you this story" (TPS005).

Another story recounted by an Elder who worked at the Faraud Hospital provides insight into the overlay of belief systems:

[The wife] had two kids, two girls, and they all died. [I'd] seen them after they were dead. [The wife] was expecting the baby to be born that's why she died [in delivery]. And she has two babies on her back [gesturing to her shoulders], two girls, they died too so we just look at them. [The nuns] want people to look at them, so they were on a stretcher bed...pulling them around the hospital to let people look.... Couldn't deliver so the mother died ... those two babies died in the womb too. So they had to take them out, they put them here [gesturing to shoulders]. So all the people has to look at it, that why they were pushing the bed around the hospital, so people can look at the lady that died with twins. (TPS008)

However, the overlay of interpretations is not complete. Whereas the traditional Tlicho perspective, described by the Elders in Whati, was that the baby needed to be taken out so that the spirit could escape (Ryan, *Traditional Dene Medicine* 238), the Christian perspective focused on the importance of removing the fetus for the purpose of baptism, to save the soul (Savona-Ventura 23). As the Faraud Hospital was a mission hospital run by nuns, it reflected not only the spiritual views Christianity informed by biblical stories but also its morality. Shari Julian discusses the story of Eve yielding to the seductions of the serpent, taking fruit from the Tree of Knowledge, and ultimately condemning Adam and all descendants to shame, hard work, painful childbirth, and suffering. Later theologians turned the story into the concept of "original sin," and with it, an eventual fear of female power and tensions about the female body (Julian 258-9; Baik-Chey 169). Eve became equated the "original sin," and the pain of childbirth became the "curse of Eve"—a phrase evident in early medical writings of women in labour (e.g., Purdy 822). The female body was seen to embody suffering. As one Tlicho woman described birth in the mission hospital with the nuns: "It was okay. They just kept praying for your suffering. Unless you were a single mother, then no needle for you" (TPS010). The moral condemnation of childbirth out of wedlock was not part of traditional Tlicho views. If a man got a woman pregnant, whether single or married, he was responsible for her and the child's wellbeing.

Although some Tlicho women had positive birth experiences at the Faraud Hospital, others were ambivalent about their experience. One Elder, who gave birth at the Faraud Hospital and later worked there, did note changing views of birth with the closure of the Faraud Hospital, and the development of the evacuation policy: "But back then every birth was successful, okay. But nowadays if they say the baby is big it can't be born they have to do cesarean;

you know, open them up and take the baby out. Back then [with the nuns] it wasn't like that. It was just successful; every child was born normal [natural birth]. Even big babies were born normal" (TPS008).

Although the "Indian problem" became medicalized with the onslaught of missionaries and the epidemics of infectious disease decimating Indigenous peoples (Waldram et al. 291), the full extent of the medicalization of birth began with the evacuation policy in the North. Closure of the "Indian hospitals" began in the 1960s, and in contrast, the number of nursing stations increased and developed as the backbone of the Medical Services Branch (198). Spiritualties, both Tlicho and Christian, eventually gave way to dominant biomedical discourse with its emphasis on technology and risk, which lead to new emplaced birth experiences and meanings inscribed on the female body.

EVACUATED BIRTH: THE FEMALE BODY AS RISK

Beginning in the 1970s and still policy today, pregnant Tlicho women, as with other Indigenous women in rural and remote communities, are evacuated at thirty-six to thirty-right weeks gestational age—according to regional policy, or sooner if a high-risk pregnancy (Lawford and Giles 327)—and brought to Yellowknife, where they must give birth. Staying in hotels, boarding homes, or with family or friends, they wait to go into labour and to be admitted to a hospital. As one Elder who was evacuated in the early 1970s recalled her experience, "I had to fly in [to Yellowknife] because the nurse, they made us fly in about a month early. So we have to stay there until, um... Long wait" (TPS002).

Being away from family and community, one Tlicho Elder re-called thinking of her mother-in-law's advice while she waited in Yellowknife:

I was staying with a friend until the baby comes. I was staying up in Yellowknife and I don't know, I eat whatever I want to eat and she had so many different kinds of food. She cooks, she bakes ... I don't know gave me heart burn,

Roman Catholic Mission and Faraud Hospital in Behchoko (original image in colour).
NWT Archives/Thomas Albert Donnelly fonds/N-2010-009: 0239

it was ever bad ... so that's the reason why I just think of my mother-in-law. If I was at home would I be like this! She always warned me. What are you eating, don't eat that. (TPS001)

As Moffitt discusses, contemporary childbirth for Tlicho women is medicalized and institutionalized predominately on risk discourse; risk informs prenatal evacuation policies (29). Consequently, the "safest birth place" becomes the hospital at the regional centre in Yellowknife. Labour and delivery in Behchoko, or one of the remote Tlicho communities, is considered to put mother and infant "at risk." Such perinatal risk factors include the following remote geographic locations with limited services; the potential for a variety of obstetrical emergencies; lack of skilled midwives perinatal nurses; neonatal problems associated with substance abuse and sexually transmitted infections (30). Although Moffitt acknowledges that there are obstetrical complications associated with birth, she emphasizes that the socially constructed risk discourse developed not in response to obstetrical emergencies but rather to scientific and technological advances, accumulated knowledge, and colonizing power (30). With advanced technology, pregnancy and birth became more of an anomaly with a narrower range of what is considered a normal pregnancy (Thachuk 49). With pregnancy no longer viewed as a natural process, the female body becomes inherently at risk.

However, Tlicho women evacuated for birth in the 1970s had not lost their belief in their traditional birth practices: "I was [in Whati] and I was ready to give birth, I was in contraction... My [mother-in-law] was with me and I was okay and I was thinking if I don't go she's going to deliver my baby. But then, um, auntie told me that [she] says I think that you're in pain, you know, you should go with the plane" (TPS001). And what is actually informing "risk" is often contested, as one Elder summed up: "I think today you know because of the expensive, and you know, it's kind of difficult for people to be travelling away from home. I think they should have midwives around just in case. You never know when the baby's gonna come" (TPS001).

Traditional knowledge and beliefs are also prevalent in the stories of younger Tlicho women that Moffitt collected in her investigation of Tlicho perinatal health beliefs and health promotion (137-69). Tlicho women aim to keep themselves well in a "world upside down" (117). The metaphor "upside down" refers to a world in conflict with traditional Tlicho values and to the trauma, isolation, and alienation resulting from colonial and assimilationist interventions into the lives and lifeways of the Tlicho. As a result Tlicho, women struggle to "keep themselves well" within their colonized world of poverty, violence, and substance abuse. Risk to maternal and perinatal health, therefore, is not inherent in the female body but rather created by the legacies of colonization and the associated intergenerational trauma.

Accordingly, Karen Lawford and Audrey Giles argue the founding goals of the evacuation policy, which have roots in the late nineteenth century, were not related to good health but attempts to assimilate and "civilize" Indigenous peoples, which led to the marginalization of Indigenous pregnancy and birth practices, and coercive pressures to adopt the Euro-Canadian's so-called superior biomedical model (327). Indigenous maternal bodies "thus became a site on which colonial goals of assimilation and civilization could be realized" (Lawford and Giles 332).

By considering birth places as embodied spaces, I reveal how colonial histories of missionization and medicalization created new emplaced birth experiences and inscribed Eurocentric meanings on Tlicho maternal bodies. Colonization became integrated into the lived experiences and rituals of birth and created birth places structured by the cultural values of the colonizer, whether saving souls or saving bodies. Evacuating Tlicho women to the "safest birth place" can be seen as removing them from their colonized communities without actually addressing key "risks" to maternal and perinatal health identified by Tlicho women. However, as Moffitt proposes, alternatively birthing in the community promises to improve perinatal health for women and their families, and allow women to have the support of family and friends and a more positive environment by fostering family unity through shared experience. Returning birth to the community would allow for traditional Tlicho customs of care by women during labour and childbirth to be revitalized and for perinatal care to be delivered in the women's language, which would afford more comfort and allow for improved knowledge transfer. Furthermore, attention to traditional practices would demonstrate respect, bolster Tlicho identity, and, in turn, improve overall health and wellness (Moffitt 117). Within this revitalized birthplace, the female body may be decolonized.

ENDNOTE

[1]To provide confidentiality, I coded the Tlicho women sharing their stories as TPS (Tlicho Pregnancy Stories) followed by a number (e.g., TPS001). The women shared their stories in English or in Tlicho with the aid of an interpreter provided by the Tlicho Government.

WORKS CITED

Baik-Chey, Soyoung. "Spirituality, Love, and Women." *Women and Christianity*, edited by Cheryl A. Kirk-Duggan and Karen

Jo Torjesen, Praeger, 2010, pp. 247-70.

Julian, Shari. "Sexuality, Politics, and Faith." *Women and Christianity*, edited by Cheryl A. Kirk-Duggan and Karen Jo Torjesen, Praeger, 2010, 165-84.

Lawford, Karen, and Audrey Giles. "Marginalization and Coercion: Canada's Evacuation Policy for Pregnant First Nations Women Who Live on Reserves in Rural and Remote Regions." *Pimatisiwin: A Journal of Aboriginal and Indigenous Community Health*, vol. 10, no. 3, 2012, pp. 327-40.

Low, Setha M. "Embodied Spaces: Anthropological Theories of Body, Space and Culture." *Space and Culture*, vol. 6, no. 1, 2003, pp. 9-18.

Moffitt, Pertice M. *'Keep Myself Well': Perinatal Health Beliefs and Health Promotion Practices among Tlicho Women*. Dissertation. University of Calgary, 2008.

Munn, Nancy D. "Excluded Spaces: The Figure in the Australian Aboriginal Landscape." *Critical Inquiry*, vol. 22, no. 3, 1996, 446-65.

Purdy, Gordon. "Women in Labour." *British Medical Journal*, vol. 1, no. 4405, 1945, pp. 822.

Ryan, Joan. *Final Report: Traditional Dene Justice Project*. Tlicho Government. 1993.

Ryan, Joan. *Final Report: Traditional Dene Medicine—Part II (Database)*. Tlicho Government. 1993.

Savona-Ventura, C. "The Influence of the Roman Catholic Church on Midwifery Practice in Malta." *Medical History*, vol. 39, no. 1, 1995, pp. 18-34.

Thachuk, Angela. "Midwifery, Informed Choice and Reproductive Autonomy: A Relational Approach." *Feminism and Psychology*, vol. 17, no. 1, 2007, pp. 39-56

Waldram, James B., et al. *Aboriginal Health in Canada*. 2nd ed.,University of Toronto Press, 2006.

9.

Maternal Identity
in Family and Community

Mothers of the Stó:lō First Nation

MARGARET MACDONALD

A S PART OF A LARGER project documenting Halq'eméylem
language revitalization (Moore and MacDonald 702),
findings from a series of in-depth interviews with eight mothers
from the Stó:lō First Nation[1] will be shared in this chapter to
illustrate maternal ties to the community and the importance of
cultural traditions to childbirth, naming practices, and maternal
identity. Our investigation into language revitalization has been
to honour and document the work taking place by the Stó:lō
and to bring important teachings forward to future generations.
The interviews discussed in this chapter, while a smaller part of
the overall project, represent an important look into maternal
practices and cultural transmission of knowledge. Narrative
themes from the interview transcripts include the following: 1)
family support, and community and cultural involvement; 2)
naming practices; and 3) cultural aspirations. Excerpts from the
interviews will illustrate the complexity of cultural transmission
and identity formation as mothers discuss their current values
and beliefs as well as the aspirations they hold for their yet to
be born or recently born children. In this chapter, I have chosen
to provide longer narrative passages to enliven the voices of the
women who participated in the interviews. Therefore, although
I have chosen the selections based on the predominant themes
immerging from the data, part of the interpretation and analysis
of the selections will rest with the reader.

Identity formation has been theorized as a dynamic interplay
between the individual and his or her social milieu (Erikson 55;

163

Stephen et al. 283; Bosma and Kunnen, 281). During adolescence identity formation is seen as the critical task of youth. They enter into a process of referencing their ideas, preferences, fears, and group uniqueness by measuring their ideals against the beliefs and values of others within and outside their social circles (Erikson 32-3; Waterma 341). In theory, these values, images, and ideals contributing to our self-identity become consolidated during such transition points across the lifespan and may also be heightened and energized by the emotions consistent with major life changes and life passages, such as school entry, puberty, school end, marriage, childbirth, retirement, and parental death (Strayer 47; Cait 87). During geographical or other transitions contributing to a change in context, "difference" can also be seen as an antecedent of identity formation. Seth Schwartz et al. (1) notes that exposure to different cultural values and systems may promote self-awareness, reflection, and consolidation that can trigger or enhance an individual's own cultural identity formation. The context of pregnancy and the transition to motherhood has also been referenced as a critical time of identity construction, given both the shifting nature of the woman's role and the transformative processes occurring during pregnancy and childbirth (Smith 281).

RESEARCH, PROCESS, AND SETTING

Permission to conduct the research informing this chapter was obtained from the Research Ethics Board at Simon Fraser University. The study design involved a purposeful sampling technique (Patton 169) of mothers visiting a Baby Time drop-in program at the Stó:lō Health Centre. Informed consent was collected from all participants. The study was explained to the mothers participating in a series of in-depth interviews (Seidman 15) about their pregnancy, their birth experience, and their aspirations for their children. These interviews were arranged at a convenient time and location for mothers, and the recordings were later transcribed and analyzed for content. For those who requested it, pseudonyms were used to ensure confidentiality.

The transcriptions yielded patterns related to the following themes: 1) family support, community, and cultural involvement;

2) naming practices, and 3) cultural aspirations. Each of these themes will be discussed as a section below using key narratives passages illustrative of values, beliefs, attitudes, and practices leading to maternal identity formation.

Within the Stó:lō territory, St Mary's Boarding School, operated by the Catholic clergy from 1863 to 1973, had a profound impact on the community. In adult testimony of their residential school experiences, members of the Stó:lō community experienced removal and placement in dormitory residence under the custodial and educational care of religious models (Carlson 68). Descriptions by members of the community vary, but typical accounts include testimony of abuse, humiliation, and threats aimed at the elimination of Halq'eméylem, their traditional language. In addition, Mary Stewart, development manager of Stó:lō Head Start Family Program, has said that because these children were separated from their families, parental modeling was also disrupted over multiple generations, which has affected either directly or indirectly all families in the community.

FAMILY AND COMMUNITY CONNECTIONS

As described above and noted elsewhere, (MacDonald 62; MacDonald et al. 183), family support within the Stó:lō community is evident in the intergenerational and community interactions taking place during gatherings, programs, or events. During the interviews, mothers mentioned the benefits of their proximity to extended family members. Family members were always referred to positively as being supportive influences in the care of their newborns, infants, and other children. At the time of the birth of their child, all the women interviewed had a great deal of intergenerational support as well as friends present either in the hospital room or waiting area. In addition to this support, all mothers mentioned their involvement in cultural events within the community prior to the birth of their child. These events included such things canoe pulling, Halq'eméylem language classes, cultural or spiritual ceremonies at the longhouse, or other Stó:lō cultural events. Typically, this participation in community events, classes and ceremonies provided mothers with exposure to cultural values

165

and traditions and community Elders who passed on advice. In the words of one mother named Carrielynne:

> Everyone wants to share their experience, and share their "dos and don'ts" and in Coast Salish culture in general,, there is a lot of superstition geared towards having a perfect baby as an outcome. So I was getting lists of things I shouldn't eat, I shouldn't do, I shouldn't say, I shouldn't look at, I shouldn't go here or go there. I'll just give a few examples. You know they would say, don't eat blueberries, don't eat strawberries or your baby will get marks on their body, and don't eat seafood, more reasons for the skin but also potential poisonings from the ocean and toxins in the ocean. Told not to cut my hair, "don't cut your hair." People said things even like don't cross your legs or your baby might get twisted inside. I was told to do a lot of walking. I participate every year in our cultural ceremonies, and I was instructed to step back from that. So it was a good chance to get to know myself again and become more familiar with my partner, spending time with him because the ceremony would be time away from him, and just a chance to take care of myself which I really hadn't done up until then, and a chance to get to know the baby of course.

PLANNING FOR BIRTH

Birth plans and positive hospital support were also referenced by several of the women in relation to their pregnancy, childbirth, and postnatal experiences. These mothers felt that the hospital personnel were accommodating of their requests to honour traditional practices, such as saving the placenta. Interestingly, the mother who described her request included a description of her family's adaptation of this traditional practice where her best girlfriend was charged by her mother to make the journey to bury the placenta instead of her husband. Another mother noted that the so-called modern birthing practice of squatting, used to increase the pelvic width, was well known as a traditional Stó:lō practice often described by family members and Elders. Mary, who had completed her nursing degree, described this blur of modern and traditional practices in the following way: "My grandma told me that they would put a rope over a branch and put it over their arms and squat because I remember in nursing school they were talking about how, "we've now discovered that if you squat it opens the pelvis up x number of inches" and I'm thinking jeez didn't my grandma tell me when I was a little girl that they have done that for years."

Four of the women described advice from their mothers, grandmothers, and Elders not to scream during childbirth, which is connected to a desire to have the baby enter into a calm world free of fear, especially the mother's fear. With pride, mother's reported they were very quiet, despite not receiving drugs for pain; they managed not to scream out. One mother, Tara, described this in detail:

> And everybody else was saying oh you're like the quietest, because everybody else was like screaming around and yelling and stuff. And then they are telling me not to be scared of that or the other girls. Cause it doesn't really help, the screaming, but I guess people just don't know what to do. But I don't know; my mom just said right from the beginning, don't go screaming around.

NAMING

All mothers mentioned having supportive husbands and the help of extended family members with decision making around naming their baby; much talk related to plans for the baby to receive what the participants referred to as their "Indian name." All babies were given first names either passed on from relatives, as in the case of two of the boys who received their father's first names, or they were given names unique in some way. For example, three of the names mentioned among boy name options were names of athletes, for example, popular hockey players (Gadin and Makita); Talus, named after a UFC fighter; and Wyze, named after a basketball player. In the latter case, following his birth much discussion took place in the hospital to determine their son's given name. Carrie-lynne describes this animated exchange:

> I liked certain old style manly names, and my partner is very creative; he's a film maker, and he considers himself to be a new eccentric philanthropist and he picked names like Solid was one of them, Shogun was another, I think Mikita, Stan Mikita he's a hockey player, so like fighter names and hockey names came up. Nitutska, which is number 1 in Blackfoot,[2] because what would we name the second one, like number 2? It was pretty ridiculous.

> But they were all very interesting names. I really liked the name Chicago, but we looked up what Chicago meant, and it means onion patch, so we weren't going to give the baby that name, but I really liked the name, and Cowboy [Carielynne's partner] liked the name as well. And Cowboy's real name is Cowboy. So he comes from a family of really creative names, his mom's name is Ticky, his name is Cowboy, his brother's name is Cheeko, but his brothers real name is Bow Tie and his sister's name is Chas. So they have very creative names, and he says our kids are not going to be Jonathan or Taylor or whatever. So I was really thinking and I had names like Edmond and Channing. I really like that style, and they are tributes to actual members of our family.

> But he didn't like any of those, and I didn't like any of his, so we decided to write equal amounts of names on two sides of the page and we got to cross off each other's. So it was like "well, I'm crossing yours off and he's like well I'm crossing this one off, well I'm crossing this one off ohhh, well I'm crossing that one off"' And we got to the bottom of the list, and there was Truth and Chicago and something that started with an S, but I can't remember what it was, I think healing power …and I remembered that I always wanted to name my first born son Wyze, and I think I saw it on the back of a basketball jersey, like it

was a basketball players last name, and it stuck with me for like ten years. Wyze and Cowboy had refused to use Truth as a middle name in any of our orders but we can use Wyze Truth, that's a beautiful name. And we were looking at him and thinking can you carry that name, and we'll call him Wyze; we'll call him Wyze Truth. I thought Truth was too much, like too much to put on his shoulders, for a first name but for a second name it would be ok. And when we are saying Truth, we're not saying be honest, so much as we're saying what truth is life, and life is unbiased, it is unsubjective it is what it is. So we are saying that is in him and in his name.

In one family, unisex names were featured for all four girls: Jordan, Jamie, Riley, and Bailey. Most of the mothers mentioned that they wanted their child's name to be unique. Four of the mothers either mentioned directly or indirectly that the Indian name the child would receive later was more significant to them than the given name because of the cultural significance that it held. All mothers wanted their baby to eventually receive an Indian name. Three of the mothers shared that they had received or were in the process of receiving Indian names themselves. This is consistent with traditions in which ancestral names (Indian names) are received later in adulthood with ceremonies varying from family to family (Thom 198). In a description of receiving his Indian name, one of the fathers, who joined his wife during the interview, reported being observed by his uncles during hunting trips, and at age fifteen, he eventually earned the name Qwpl/stum, Great Hunter—a name carried by his Uncle and passed on to him by his great grandfather. He described the experience as such:

I started hunting when I was eight years old. I'd go out and I'd help my grandpa uncles and my dad. We'd drag the deer or help skin it, I cut the meat. Until I was able to handle a firearm and uh then I started. I think I shot my first deer when I was twelve. I didn't know that my grandfather and my uncle were really watching me and I didn't know I was earning that right. They said I did enough to earn that

name. They kind of blessed me with that name—Qwpl/
stum James George.

When asked if he was going to be watching his son, James Jr. in
the same way, James Sr. commented "I actually want to share my
name with him [earlier] so he can grow with it and understand it
while he's young. And I can encourage him to follow those ways."
The importance of having a son to share the name was very emotional for James and Audrey who explained that it meant a great
deal to them.

> Audrey: There's a lot of time we had to think about what
> we want for him since we had ultra sound. And when she
> said that to us at the ultra sound, she says "oh it's a little
> boy, we can see a little thingy on there." We were just like
> so happy. It didn't matter to me if I had a boy or a girl,
> but it meant a lot to have a son because I already had a
> daughter.
> James: And it just made us cry we were so happy.
>
> Audrey: Mmhm. He already had his name picked out even
> before we knew he was a boy [laughing]
>
> James: It was like a … like a… [tears] like a dream for me
> to have a junior. Someone to be like me but better.

ASPIRATIONS

Among cultural aspirations for their children, all mothers mentioned
that they wanted their children to learn Halq'eméylem and to
take part in the same cultural activities that they do or those their
husbands take part in. This included participation in longhouse
events for those whose families participated, and traditional athletic
events such canoe racing. For example, in addition to giving James
Jr. his ancestral name, James and Audrey discussed other cultural
aspirations that they had for James Jr., including being involved
with both the winter and summer dances. James Sr. explained it
in the following way:

We want him to learn both. We follow two traditions. I'm kind of involved in the longhouse, the winter dance, and plus we follow the summer dance too, the powwows. I want to get him into to dancing, and if he gets older then he can sing too. I sing right now but I want to dance. A lady passed on her headdress to me and uh that's a big honour. Someday, he'll wear it too.

Mothers who were given regalia—or had made them for their sons or daughters to use in the powwow for grass dances or jingle dancing—wanted their children to be involved in the powwow. Other mothers mentioned that they saw the powwow as a possible option if their children became interested in it or as a way to learn about other First Nations cultures, but they felt that it was not central to their own family traditions and would be more peripheral to their aspirations for their children. One mother commented that it would be like exposing her daughter to a new sport, but she did not necessarily see it as being culturally significant to her family. As explained by Verly Ned, the powwow is a modern cultural adaptation within the Stó:lō community: "the Powwow wasn't in our area ... Different families got married into people back east and they started to bring in the Powwow [to Chilliwack]."

Throughout this project, we have observed shifts in which the traditional teachings of the Elders are now augmented in different ways with direct teaching of protocols and cultural traditions in intergenerational family programs (i.e., the Stó:lō Nation Head Start Program). Halq'eméylem language teacher Seliselwet Bibiana Norris explained this in the following way:

Our grandparents and parents took us as a family to the longhouse so that we could learn the teachings and protocols of our culture. The most important thing for us to do as children in the longhouse was to listen and be very quiet so that we would hear the teachings. The strictness with which I was raised was not so much traditional for our people as it was the result of the training that our Elders received as children in residential schooling. Despite this restrictive upbringing, I have found alternative ways of teaching the cultural expectations to my children and to others.... when I am teaching a drum song to a group of students, I make my voice clear with the anticipation that the students will want to listen and learn.

Knowing my cultural teachings gives me a true sense of my identity and gives me the confidence to be a strong person. In my culture, the women are the backbone of the society. Our family structures are matrilineal since time immemorial. Prior to European influences when a woman married, her husband joined her family and left his own. Raiders from other Nations would come to steal the women folk so that they could build strength within their Nation. Women of my culture have always had to be very strong in order to assist their families.

My immediate family always comes first in my life followed my extended family and my friends. People call on me to help them with their difficulties by speaking up for them during meetings, and family conferences. I am also asked to speak on behalf of others at funerals, in the longhouse and when working with people who are influenced adversely by drug and alcohol abuse.... I believe that my strength comes from my cultural teachings. Being aware of these teachings makes me feel rich and well cared for so that is the strength that I try to pass on to others especially my children.

CONCLUSION

Conceptually, identifying the way that culture contributes to identity formation can be challenging, given the difficulty of pin pointing where one culture begins and another ends. Global or popular culture as evidenced in the use of technology, mass media, or food standardization is by definition ubiquitous and has inevitable influence upon individual, family, or community culture. This blurring of cultures in concert with Jerome Bruner's (116) view that "self" is defined by "both by the individual and the culture in which he or she participates" points toward a recursive reflective transmission of culture. This helps to contest the notion of culture as a fixed entity (Schwartz 3) and directs us toward a view of self and culture as constructed through negotiated understandings that vary within and across individual and social contexts (school, community, family setting etc.). This heuristic or way of knowing—that describes the construction of self and culture as a recursive and reflective process—has been adopted within this research project as a way to better understand the experiences of the mothers participating in these interviews. Each mother's past experiences, development, and individual characteristics all contribute to her construction of maternal identity and culture, which are influenced by the broader values and belief systems embedded in the contexts that she operates within. Importantly, these constructions also influence culture, as decisions are negotiated and agreed upon regarding cultural aspirations and the pathways that she and her family take. As stated by Bruner, "in some sense we are 'creatures of history,' in another sense we are autonomous agents as well" (110). In these ways, we are influenced by the maternal identity of the past but also creators of maternal identity, as we negotiate and construct, produce and consume the cultures we operate within.

Taken together, pregnancy and childbirth considered within the Stó:lō cultural milieu embody all the elements of what Edgar Morin refers to as "human complexity." The experience described by these mothers is illustrative of what Morin refers to as the part in the whole and the whole in the part (Morin 75) where the birth of a child, is the birth and continuation also of our cultural transmission. This critical life passage is the hallmark of "joint development of individual autonomies, community participation and a sense of belonging to the human species," a triad that Morin refers to as the elements of human complexity (*Seven*, 45). This parallels the teachings of the Stó:lō and is consistent with their understanding of time. As Keith Carlson explains:

> In Halq'eméylem the term *tómiyeqw* is used to express the relationships of great-great-great-great-grandparent, great-great-great-great-granduncle/aunt, great-great-great-great-grandchild and great-great-great-great-grandniece/

nephew. In this way, people from parallel past and future generations up to seven times removed from current living relatives are considered to hold the same relationship with the current living generation. (28)

For these reasons, interviews with mothers who have had these recent child birth experiences and who are members of a distinct cultural community are particularly insightful given the contribution they make to our understanding of cultural transmission and identity formation and ways that the past and present experiences have been woven together.

ENDNOTES

[1]The Stó:lō First Nation is made up of eleven bands located along the upper Fraser River in the Fraser Valley, approximately two hundred kilometres outside Greater Vancouver, British Columbia (see https://en.wikipedia.org/wiki/Sto:lo.).
[2]Carrilynne's husband is a member of the Blackfoot Nation from the Edmonton area.

WORKS CITED

Bosma, Harke, and E. Saskia Kunnen. "Identity-in-Context Is Not Yet Identity Development-in-Context." *Journal of Adolescence*, vol. 31, no. 2, 2008, pp. 281-89.

Bruner, Jerome. *Acts of Meaning*. Harvard University Press, 1990.

Cait, Cheryl-Anne. "Parental Death, Shifting Family Dynamics, and Female Identity Development." *Omega*, vol. 51, no. 2, 2005, pp. 87-105.

Carlson, Keith Thor, editor. *A Stó:lō Coast Salish Historical Atlas.* Douglas and McIntyre, 2001.Erikson, Erik. *The Life Cycle Completed*. Norton. 1997.

MacDonald, Margaret. "Halq'eméylem Language Revitalization: Walking in Both Worlds." *Native Studies Review*, vol. 18, no. 2, 2009, pp. 62-77.

MacDonald, Margaret, et al. "Elders, Family, Teachers: Models in Stó:lō Cultural Transmission." *Child Health and Education*, vol. 1, no. 4, 2009, pp. 183-205.

Morin, Edgar. *Seven Complex Lessons in Education for the Future.* UNESCO Publishing. 2001.

Moore, Daniéle, and Margaret MacDonald. "Language and Literacy Development in a Canadian Native Community: Halq'eméylem Revitalization in a Stó:lō Head Start Program in British Columbia." *The Modern Language Journal*, vol. 97, no. 3, 2013, pp. 702-19.

Ned, Verly. Personal interview. April 2007.

Norris, Bibiana. Personal interview. 21 Jan. 21 2008.

Patton, Michael Q. *Qualitative Evaluation Methods.* Sage. 1990.

Schwartz, Seth J., et al. "The Role of Identity in Acculturation among Immigrant People: Theoretical Propositions, Empirical Questions, and Applied Recommendations." *Human Development*, vol. 49, 2006, pp. 1-30.

Seidman, Irving. *Interviewing as Qualitative Research: A Guide for Researchers in Education and the Social Sciences.* 3rd ed. Teachers College Press, 2006.

Smith, Johnathan A. "Identity Development During the transition to Motherhood." *Journal of Reproductive and Infant Psychology*, vol. 17.no. 3, 1999, 281-98.

Strayer, Janet. "The Dynamics of Emotions and Life Cycle Identity." *Identity: An International Journal of Theory and Research*, vol. 2, no. 1, 2002, pp. 47-79.

Stephen, Joanne, et al. "Moratorium-Achievement (Mama) Cycles in Lifespan Identity Development: Value Orientations and Reasoning System Correlates." *Journal of Adolescence*, vol. 15, no. 3, 1992, pp. 283-300.

Stewart, Mary. Personal interview. May 2009.

Thom, Brian. "Coast Salish Senses of Place: Dwelling, Meaning, Power, Property and Territory in the Coast Salish World." Dissertation, McGill University. 2005.

10.
Indigenous Birth in Canada

Reconciliation and Reproductive Justice
in the Settler State

ERIKA FINESTONE AND CYNTHIA STIRBYS

Over twenty years ago, the 1996 Final Report of the Royal Commission of Aboriginal Peoples (RCAP) stated, "there is a growing convergence between Aboriginal and non-Aboriginal perspectives on what make people healthy. Indeed, some Aboriginal communities are on the leading edge of innovations in this area. This suggested improved collaboration might be mutually beneficial" (RCAP 10). Two decades have passed and though collaborative efforts between Indigenous and non-Indigenous stakeholders exist, an imbalance of power in favour of Western ontologies still punctuates many of these relationships. With the collaborative writing of this chapter we the authors—one Saulteaux-Cree[1] scholar and the other a settler scholar[2]—attempt to identify where and how new relational convergences can foster mutually beneficial changes in our communities. We are connected and propelled by our shared desire to advance Indigenous reproductive justice in Canada as one necessary component of a broader decolonizing and reconciliatory project in the settler state.

We come together as women,[3] both at our core seeking further freedom of choice, freedom of being, and freedom of thought in a colonial context oppressive to *all woman* (albeit in different ways and with different consequences).[4] We hope that by critically engaging with the history of childbirth in Canada, we can better understand the particular ways in which Indigenous birth has been challenged by patriarchal policies and practices. At the same time, we hope to open space for dialogue and further inquiry into the ways in which we, as women of varying backgrounds, both settler and Indigenous, have been at once privileged *and* oppressed throughout this history of birth and into the present. By framing the chapter in this way, we aim to experiment with the creation of an "ethical space of engagement"[5] wherein Indigenous and non-Indigenous women can begin to imagine new possibilities for a less violent system within which all women can safely bring new life onto these lands.

INTRODUCTION

This chapter emerges from its intellectual gestation at a point in time when Indigenous women around the globe are tirelessly seeking reproductive justice by standing up for the right to practice their own birth and childcare ceremonies. Reproductive justice can be defined as "the right to have children, not have children, and parent the children we have in safe and healthy environments—[and] is based on the human right to make personal decisions about one's life, and the obligation of government and society to ensure that the conditions are suitable for implementing one's decisions" (qtd. in Hoover et al. 1645). This movement toward reproductive justice exists on multiple sociopolitical levels; it is at once a struggle to reclaim Indigenous birth practices and sovereignty over the family; a demand for customary rights and emerging forms of matriarchy; and a movement toward self-determination and community resurgence. The reclamation of Indigenous birth is *not* a struggle for recognition by the Canadian state. It is *not* a struggle for cultural preservation to salvage a disappearing tradition. A movement toward Indigenous birth does not occur in opposition to the settler state and its desires or values; it stands alone and involves the resurgence of ceremonies and practices that, at their core, assert the futurity of Indigenous peoples by honouring the very first environments—the mother's womb (Cook 79).

This chapter begins by giving a brief history of some of the key challenges to Indigenous pregnancy and birth in the settler colonial context in the lands commonly known as "Canada." We then move on to some of the contemporary challenges faced by Indigenous communities when it comes to maintaining Indigenous birth practices in settler colonies. Specifically, we highlight some of the work being brought to life by Indigenous scholars and community advocates, many of whom are investing their time and energy into advancing Indigenous reproductive justice in Canada. In the following pages, we aim to interrogate the layers of meaning, conflict, and opportunity associated with the joining of the terms "Indigenous" and "birth" into ideology and praxis. We will ask the following: what makes Indigenous birthing practices distinct from other birth methods? How does Indigenous birth stand alone as a decolonial project, and how does it become part of the broader politics of pregnancy, birth, motherhood, and childrearing in settler states? These questions, and others, will be incubated in the sections below.

HISTORICAL CHALLENGES TO INDIGENOUS BIRTH MODELS AND INDIGENOUS MIDWIFERY

The RCAP Report offers several recommendations aiming to "restore justice to the relationship between Aboriginal and non-Aboriginal people in Canada" (1). The report asserts that policies put in place by the Canadian government to "heal" Indigenous Peoples are often well intentioned but "wrong for the job" (1). Specifically, the RCAP Report highlights that Indigenous Peoples' health is based on "the connectedness of human systems," the environment in which healthcare is administered, and "personal responsibility" over health, which Indigenous Peoples determine is "as important as professional expertise" (5-6).[6]

Good intentions alone have not alleviated the health discrepancies between Indigenous communities and the rest of Canada. In fact, the recommendations RCAP intended to put into practice still hold relevance now as they resurface in the 2015 Final Report of the Truth and Reconciliation Commission of Canada (TRC). The report stresses that "Indigenous peoples have the right to be actively involved in developing, determining, and administering health programs that affect them" (207), and also "have the right to traditional medicines and to maintain their traditional health practices" (207). The TRC calls upon "those who can affect change within the Canadian health-care system to recognize the value of Aboriginal healing practices and use them in the treatment of

Aboriginal patients in collaboration with Aboriginal healers and Elders where requested by Aboriginal patients" (210).

When it comes to reproductive rights, one of the central challenges in honouring the TRC's commitment is the fact that birth practices do not fall comfortably within the realm of "healing practices"; pregnant Indigenous women do not require a cure or "treatment" for symptoms. Indigenous women will give birth, will give life, and will bring forth a new member of the community. This is a process of gifting, not of removal. A gift necessarily requires a receiver, whether a community member, a midwife, a friend, or even the labouring woman herself. The gift of birth should not (in most cases) require a healer or medical practitioner, only a supporter. This explanation may seem redundant, but pregnant women have been pathologized and birth medicalized to such an extent in Euroamerican societies that this reconceptualization of birth, not as a procedure but as a sacred gifting process, is a necessary rearticulation.

Midwives are crucial receivers in Indigenous birth, and active agents of the Indigenous reproductive justice movement. Paramount to many Indigenous birthing practices, the role of the midwife is to provide education in maternal, family, and community health (NAHO, "Midwifery" 4-5). Traditionally and contemporarily, an Indigenous midwife coaches women on lifestyle changes in addition to creating programming pertaining to diet, home life, substance-use challenges, and emotional and spiritual wellbeing. As such, Indigenous midwives provide a holistic support system to pregnant women throughout the childbearing cycle (Midwives of Sudbury).

Women's traditional practice as healers and midwives was a respected vocation wherein women primarily supported women during childbirth, not just for the benefit of the birthing mother, but to provide female caregivers the opportunity to apprentice with more experienced midwives (NAHO, "Midwifery" 5; Anderson 48). From this apprenticeship, younger women learned about the "*people's* medicine" from the older midwives (Ehrenreich and English 22, emphasis in original). Overall, birth was a time for women to honour and celebrate the "prodigious power" they held as life givers (Corea 303).

Challenges to maintain Indigenous birth practices began soon after settlers arrived with new ideas of health and the female body. In the early twentieth century, philanthropic foundations, such as the Carnegie and Rockefeller Institutes, gave financial backing to create a medical profession excluding women; thus, the new sciences and technology were only allowed for use by male physicians who propagated their superiority over not only midwives but "the mystique of women [pregnancy]" (Stirbys "Without" 3). The eventual decline of the midwife's role began with the patriarchal notion that women did not have the intellect to practice medicine (NAHO, "Midwifery"). Medicine was for male practitioners only, who eventually transformed obstetrics into a "lucrative business" (Ehrenreich and English 20). With the newly established medical profession, male physicians campaigned against midwifery and claimed it was unsafe because midwives lacked formal medical training (20). Ironically, midwives taught medical students about pregnancy and birth at McGill University in Canada until the late 1880s (NAHO, "Midwifery"). Nonetheless, discrediting midwifes had "more to do with business, politics and economics than developing new and innovative ways to reliably secure the safety of mothers and children" (Stirbys, "Without" 3).

Changing attitudes toward midwifery continue to affect Indigenous women's access to birth plans rooted in their communities' customs and practices. Although midwifery was once "the customary, respected practice even among the colonists," with the creation of the medical profession physicians began almost unanimously promoting biomedical-birthing interventions over midwifery (NAHO, "Midwifery" 7). At this time, physicians were relegating Indigenous knowledge of childbirth to the past, as something not quite on par with the scientific and technological advances of the medical profession; they framed Indigenous birth methods as 'risky' by comparison. According to many Indigenous peoples, this formula for biomedical risk has contributed to the design of government policies and legislation that "undermine their collective sense of identity" and chips away at their "right to be self-governing, self-determining peoples" (Canada, RCAP 23). Overall, Indigenous birthmothers in Canada have "come under increasing surveillance and ideological control" since colonization

(Fordyce and Maraesa 1), and their reproductive freedoms continue to be threatened under these conditions today.

CONTEMPORARY CHALLENGES TO
INDIGENOUS BIRTH MODELS

Indigenous women seeking customary birth methods in their communities may face many challenges. Primary amongst them is the dominant ideology that giving birth in community with the help of a midwife alone puts them at risk of "reproductive danger" (Fordyce and Maraesa 1). This fear mongering around reproductive risk has fuelled the development of medical policies, public health campaigns, and development initiatives that claim to mediate these risks (Fordyce and Maraesa 1). For instance, in the early 1970s, the federal government began implementing the policy of "evacuation" requiring that all pregnant women residing in "isolated and under populated northern areas of Canada travel to urban hospitals in the south, several weeks before their expected due date" (Bourgeault et al. 3).

Although this practice was framed as a way of "mediating risk," it has been reported that forced evacuations have resulted in the "breakup of families, the loss of community knowledge about birth, and health problems [for] women who must sit for weeks in southern cities waiting to go into labour, with strange food, little exercise and no family support" (Daviss 445). This process has been most traumatically felt in Inuit communities, where there was once a "near obliteration of their childbirth practices" (Stirbys, "Without" 16). For the Inuit this has become a "focus of political, community, and personal outrage" (16).

Tr'ondëk Hwëch'in scholar Rachel Olson argues a link exists between the advancement of colonization and practices designed to control the bodies of Indigenous women (Olson 178):

I see that taking the job of midwives and moving birth into the hospital is something that is akin to colonization.... Most non-native people, and even some native people, would see this as just something about modern life. But I am not convinced and I don't think I will ever be convinced, that we needed to have modern life that much…Just like taking our land, they took our bodies. And they used women's bodies. And we can look at that through history, that this was the way people conquered…conquered the land, conquered the people…[I]t wasn't always negative, but I think in the case of birth it did become negative, because we [midwives] were made useless. (178)

Policies removing birthmothers from their communities as a means of mediating risk are a classic example of the self-congratulatory efforts of the settler state to save Indigenous peoples from their own so-called risky practices (Ross; Di Tomasso and de Finney). These impositions into traditional birth practices have wide-ranging and long-term effects. Giving birth outside of one's community could mean the loss of crucial opportunities for mother-child bonding, a missed opportunity for intergenerational knowledge exchanges surrounding birth, and the inability to perform ritualistic postpartum practices involving the mother, newborn, the extended family, and the land (Schwarz; Andersen; Simpson). Of particular concern, many stories tell of Indigenous women (often those who have open child welfare cases) being forced into the hospital setting to give birth only to have their newborn apprehended by a child protection agent and placed in care immediately thereafter.[7]

Such instances remind us that another set of risk factors linger long after a so-called safe hospital birth: the psychological and emotional risks associated with a loss of freedom over one's body; the risk of losing one's child to the system; the risk of cultural erasure and identity loss for mother and child. In the next section, we explore the multitudinous effects of an extractive approach to childbirth vis-à-vis a discussion of Urie Bronfenbrenner's adapted socioecological model.

THE INDIGENOUS SOCIOECOLOGICAL BIRTH MODEL

The TRC and RCAP reports clearly outline that Indigenous communities have the right to access and practice their customs and/or traditions. Despite the political and constitutional recognition of

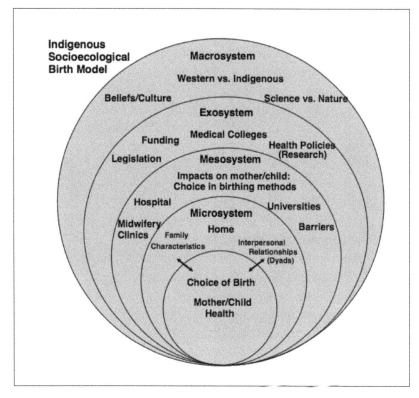

Indigenous customs, the state continues to intrude upon Indigenous women's sovereignty over the birth process. This signals a possible disjuncture between the politics of recognizing Indigenous customs and understandings of the practical forms these customs take in contemporary contexts (Coulthard; Povinelli). In this section, we will discuss some of the nuances of Indigenous birth customs that, at times, markedly challenge dominant Euroamerican birth models.

To illustrate these differences, Dr. Stirbys adapted Bronfenbrenner's socioecological model[8] (Bronfenbrenner and Crouter; Bronfenbrenner) through an Indigenous reproductive justice lens (Hoover et al.; SisterSong; Gurr; Weibe) now named the "Indigenous Socioecological Birth Model." Using the model, the benefits of a Western biomedical approach to birth can be measured next to Indigenous birth values[9] by calling attention to contextual issues such as the birthmother's family and community and the external and internal forces affecting them: social, spiritual, cultural, environmental, political, and beyond. We hope this model can be used as a tool to assist in the development of appropriate protocols and practices that honour, as opposed to undermine, Indigenous women's experience of pregnancy, birth, and motherhood in settler states.

The Indigenous Socioecological Birth Model consists of four concentric circles encompassing the different variables affecting the choices and health of an expectant mother and child: the "microsystem," "mesosystem," "exosystem," and "macrosystem." The four levels of the model are also individually and collectively impacted by a temporal dimension called the "chronosystem" (not pictured in model).

The macrosystem represents the cultural, geopolitical, and economic context constructing different belief systems. This level allows one to reflect on the different approaches to childbirth resulting from diverse worldviews and cultural practices. Whereas a dominant Western worldview sees medical intervention and technology as a common component of childbirth, the Indigenous worldview promotes choice, whereby the woman controls where and how she will birth—whether that be with the assistance of a midwife, a doctor, or otherwise.

The exosystem acknowledges the societal context in which a decision maker is situated, but specifically refers to the factors an individual cannot directly control. It highlights the societal structures impacting the scope of possibilities available to the decision maker, such as the availability of and funding for community services and agencies devoted to childbirth, or the policies and/or laws related to birth. The exosystem often determines the extent to which a woman can access different birth options. The availability of diverse birth options or practices varies greatly between Indigenous communities, especially when communities are more remote (i.e., further from a metropolitan centre) and/or socioeconomically strained. In other cases, discrepancies between Indigenous traditions and provincial laws and/or policies surrounding birth affect women's access to alternative options, such as midwifery and homebirths. When considering Indigenous reproductive justice, it is important to remember that "the ability of a woman to determine her reproductive destiny is in many cases directly tied to conditions in her community" (qtd.

in Hoover et al. 1646). These issues and their outcomes will be discussed further in the coming sections.

The innermost circle is the microsystem, which makes up the immediate social context of Indigenous expectant mothers, including interpersonal relationships, and/or the activities and roles she and her primary supporters take on. These relationships, or 'primary dyads,' consist of two people emotionally significant to each other (Bronfenbrenner). Included in the Indigenous Socioecological Birth Model's microsystem are the mother-child dyad; the mother-father dyad; the midwife-mother dyad; and the mother-other-members-of-the-extended-family dyad, which can include aunties, grandmother, friends, and children. In an Indigenous birth model, relationship building with the extended kin (both biological and relational) is central to creating a safe space for the expectant mother. As such, the midwife (or any chosen birth-supporter) considers the needs of both the mother and the family when developing an individualized birth plan.

Falling between the exosystem and microsystem is the mesosystem, which accounts for the connections between multiple microsystems (Bronfenbrenner). This level considers the potential outcomes of bridging two microsystems, and the effect this can have on the birth plan, and/or the health of mother and baby. For instance, imagine a midwife-mother dyad (one microsystem) has a meeting with an important member-of-the-extended-family, such as the maternal grandmother (another microsystem). This bridging of two microsystems has the potential to be a positive experience for all participants. Perhaps the grandmother gets along well with the midwife and becomes an active member of their birth support network; this reinforces the mother's birth choices and escalates her chances of having a minimally stressful, healthy birth. Alternatively, perhaps the grandmother does not approve of the midwife and, as such, disrupts the midwife-mother dyad; she calls her birth plan into question and creates stress negatively affecting mom and baby. This example speaks to the importance of good communication, consent, and cooperation between microsystems during the birth cycle in order to advance mother and child health.

The temporal dimension known as the chronosystem considers the historical factors or political climate that may have impacted the birthmother or the members of their support network. The chronosystem surrounds all levels of the socioecological model from micro to macro, symbolizing that historical context has a profound effect on all levels of the system. Contextualizing the chronosystem through an Indigenous lens requires a shift away from Western notions of personhood and corporeality. Whereas Western thought sees land and body as distinct (hierarchically positioning humans above nature), many Indigenous societies believe the memories and substance of lived experience are held in the land itself; in this sense, the land has a spirit inextricable from the bodies of Indigenous peoples occupying it. This relationship between land and body crosses generational boundaries in a spiritual flow of time. The history and memory of birth is therefore felt in the fibres of the land on which the mother performs this act, which nurtures the body and spirit of her surrounding community and all the living things within it. Birth is a ceremony binding Indigenous life to the land.

Because of the connective force between an Indigenous birthmother and land, any policies or practices disrupting this connection are extremely problematic, and can leave a lasting mark on the chronosystem of which the mother, child, and community are a part. For this reason, the systematic dislocation of Indigenous life givers from their traditional territories[10] (or whichever community they call home) represents a direct assault on Indigenous spirits, bodies, lands, and relations. Any fissure in the sacred relationship between birth, memory, and land affects all levels of the socioecological model and, by extension, the long-term health of Indigenous families and communities.

In sum, the Indigenous Socioecological Birth Model illustrates the importance of considering all factors—social, historical, political, economic, relational, geographic, and spiritual—affecting a birthmother's decision-making process or the degree to which she can access different birth options. With these multileveled considerations in mind, it becomes easier to comprehend how challenges that may seem quite minor in any one level of the model can have a trickle-down effect and become sizable barriers to Indigenous reproductive justice. The model also shows the redundancy of policy changes seeking to break down one barrier to Indigenous birth through a Band-Aid approach while failing to address its root causes. In the following section, we explore how the current power relations at work in the Canadian settler state affect the different levels of the Indigenous Socioecological Birth Model.

INDIGENOUS BIRTH AND RECOGNITION POLITICS IN CANADA

Acknowledging the interdependence of the levels in the Indigenous Socioecological Birth Model, we must question policies claiming to recognize Indigenous self-determination over birth, while upholding systems creating barriers within or between its levels. As Elizabeth Povinelli importantly points out, the "cunning" of state recognition in settler colonies is that although the state seemingly acknowledges Indigenous ways of life, it tactfully skirts around the issue of "the potential radical alterity of Indigenous beliefs, practices, and social organization" (163). Indigenous birth customs are often only recognized insofar as they do not disturb medicalized standards for proper birth practices as per the dominant Canadian nation state's macrosystem. In place of policies recognizing the nuances of Indigenous birth customs, the state more often uplifts customary practices deemed acceptable within their existing standards for "Good and Right practices" (163).

Take for instance the "Aboriginal Birthing Strategy" (ABS)—an initiative of the Society of Obstetricians and Gynaecologists (SOGC)—created with the goal of generating "action to improve the health of Aboriginal children, to address health inequities and create a framework for comprehensive, collaborative partnerships" (NAHO "Celebrating Birth" 26). The ABS highlights, among other goals, the importance of developing "culturally sensitive practices" and "listening to women's voices" (27). These are, without a doubt, two important focus areas when it comes to improving Indigenous women's contemporary experience of pregnancy and birth. However, other areas of the document are still arguably written in the language of biomedicine, with an emphasis on mediating the perceived risks of childbirth through "standardized curriculums" for midwives (27). Framing the goals of the ABS in this way continues to emphasize the importance of professionalization as a "safety measure", which, ironically, was exactly the discourse that historically undermined the credibility of midwives.

Not surprisingly, Indigenous customary practices officially recognized by the Canadian government are often the least transgressive and the most tokenistic, yet they are often touted as examples of Canada's admirable adherence to the value of multiculturalism. When it comes to Indigenous customary birth practices, these efforts to gain state recognition may inadvertently trivialize Indigenous traditions. For instance, prior to colonial contact when,

> midwives lived a distance away from where the delivery was to take place, it was often necessary for her to move in with the expectant mother. Living with the mother fostered an extended model of care.... By moving in with the families or being in close proximity, the midwives were able to help with prenatal and postnatal care as well as infant care. (Anderson 48)

Today, the First Nations Inuit Health Branch (FNIHB), an arm of Health Canada, proposed to work with Aboriginal Peoples, provinces, and territories as part of an initiative to return safe birthing closer to communities (FNIHB). Although the FNIHB's strategy represents an attempt to bridge Canadian and Indigenous health priorities, their goals do not holistically address the issue of proximity, intimacy, and long-term care between Indigenous birthmothers and birth supporters. For many Indigenous Peoples, the goal is not to bring birthing *closer* to but actually *back* to their communities, which follows the chronosystem's emphasis on birth, land, and memory. Therefore, a closer examination of the values underpinning traditional birth models may be necessary to inform new policies and programs that can better meet the needs of Indigenous birthmothers and their communities.

In another act of recognition that misses the mark, though the federal government has now recognized midwifery as, at minimum, a tolerated form of birth-assistance in Canada, this courtesy has not yet been extended to Indigenous midwives (Stirbys, "Explaining," "Without"). By extension, there is little (and in some provinces no) government funding for Indigenous midwifery clinics, and in all but three provinces, there is no provincial legislation under which Indigenous midwifery falls[11]; consequentially, there are relatively few Indigenous midwifery clinics in Canada.[12] Existing Aboriginal midwifery clinics mostly offer a hybridized version of Indigenous practices "complemented" by so-called "*modern* forms of medical care" (Skye 32, emphasis added). Although these Indigenous midwifery centres may be safe spaces for a number of Indigenous mothers, the tendency to position Indigenous birth practices as antiquated in relation to modern midwifery styles remains problematic. As well, because of their limited number, these clinics do not currently represent a holistic or even viable solution to the risk of evacuated birth.

The general attitude that outside intervention is a common-sense response to Indigenous birthmothers' current challenges foregoes more long-term investment in, and capacity building for the development of community-led, culturally relevant birth options. This issue is salient in underserviced and remote communities, but it also applies to a growing number of urban Indigenous peoples requiring birth supports as well. The tendency of settler governments to extract from rather than invest in Indigenous communities is easily visible in policies such as evacuated birth, but it does not stand alone; it can be categorized alongside a whole host of other Canadian social policies that (though at times well-intentioned) simply bandage up structural issues instead of treating root problems. A more critical and specific assessment of the different barriers (financial, emotional, familial, and geographic) preventing Indigenous birthmothers from accessing safe birth options will be necessary if we are to approach this issue in a trauma-informed, long-term, and anticolonial way.

Moving forward, we must think critically not only about the alliances built to advocate for Indigenous birthmothers but the operative language used to describe the changes being sought. The labelling of Indigenous birthmothers as risky, or calling their birth practices premodern, reflects a blaming logic that first victimizes and then seeks to save Indigenous bodies, often under the guise of reconciliation. Breaking down barriers to Indigenous women's access to their own birth practices requires assessing where colonial traces linger in current health policies and making them visible for what they often are: instances of obstetric violence[13] diminishing Indigenous women's reproductive freedoms. Indigenous scholars and activists play a hugely important role in naming and critiquing instances where reconciliation and recognition politics overshadow the decolonizing of birth in Canada. These actors are responding with powerful alternatives—some of which will be explored below.

INDIGENOUS RESISTANCE TO THE ERASURE
OF INDIGENOUS BIRTH

In *Defamiliarizing the Aboriginal: Cultural Practices and Decolonization in Canada*, Julia Emberley argues that colonial policies were originally put in place to "regulate the bodies of Indigenous women by controlling their sexual, reproductive, and kinship relations" (47). The reproductive body was and remains a crucial component of colonial and neocolonial governance. Advocates for Indigenous peoples' reproductive justice are, therefore, not only resisting the state's encroachment on the domain of birth, but also the larger colonial project of Indigenous erasure. This section showcases some scholarship that challenges the state's attempts to further control and confine Indigenous families by theorizing about and modeling contemporary approaches to Indigenous birth in settler states.

Michi Saagiig Nishnaabeg scholar Leanne Simpson contends a resurgence of Indigenous pregnancy, birth, and childrearing creates a foundation for sustained Indigenous nationhood. Simpson asks us to picture the Indigenous family as the "teaching ground" (L. Simpson 106) for the building of positive relationships between peoples and nations. These teachings are actualized, in part, through the "everyday acts" of mother and child (L. Simpson; Corntassel et al., forthcoming). For instance, the relationship between breastfeeding and treaty making may not be immediately obvious. Simpson, however, sees the act of breastfeeding as providing the very first teaching of reciprocity between two peoples, which sets the stage for relationships between nations (106). She argues the following: "Nursing is ultimately about a relationship. Treaties are ultimately about a relationship. One is a relationship based on sharing between a mother and child and the other based on sharing between two sovereign nations" (107). By magnifying breastfeeding as a practice through which anti-imperialist relationships are built, Simpson illustrates the importance of the mother-child dyad being honoured as a model for healthy nation-building spiraling outward from the microsystem.[14]

Indigenous women across Turtle Island are coming together to signal the importance of women's bodies as the "first environments" for community growth. Cree lawyer, judge, and legislative advocate for children's rights Marie Ellen Turpel-Lafond argues that "It is women who give birth both in the physical and in the spiritual sense to the social, political, and cultural life of the community" (qtd. in Emberley 55). From this point of view, fertility and motherhood are not taken-for-granted aspects of a gendered life course but are inextricably linked to an Indigenous nation-building project reliant on the activities of women. Leanne Simpson adds: "By reclaiming pregnancy and birth, we are not only physically decolonizing ourselves but we are also providing a decolonized pathway into this world. It is our responsibility to the next generation" (28). As such, Indigenous birth secures the futurity of Indigenous communities and is, therefore, an inherently decolonial practice. By extension, we must remain critical of colonial policies couched in the language of recognition that deliberately or inadvertently "undermine [Indigenous women's] sacred responsibilities as life-givers" (Couchie and Nabigon 41-43; Patel and Al-Jazairi 55).

Evacuated birth and other extractive policies further the colonial enterprise by erasing Indigenous presences from their land. In the language of the socioecological model, these processes disrupt the chronosystem where the memory of birth is spiritually and physically invested in land and community. Resisting this form of erasure, Cherokee scholar Jeff Corntassel describes his own experience renewing a birth ceremony in a settler-colonial context. He writes,

> After [my daughter] was born, the nurses saved the birth cord and placenta for me in the refrigerator. I froze it for several months while thinking of a plan for how to return it to Cherokee territory ... I wanted to motivate her to go home and feel what it's like to walk among our ancestors... to breathe in and connect with the land so deeply that you can't imagine your life without it. When my daughter was

older, I showed her where it was buried in Oklahoma, and she remembers. Through a process of renewal (retelling and regenerating this story and actions that go with it), she embodies her relational responsibilities. This is where people, place and practices converge. (Corntassel et al. np.)

Corntassel offers, by way of conclusion, "When talking about everyday, we have these new stories to share on new ways we re-engaged with our traditions." By recounting this "living history" (np) of a postpartum land-based ceremony, Corntassel is activating Indigenous resurgence. Such stories, lived, told, and embodied in place, represent an investment in the futurity of Indigenous Peoples on lands where their presence is often erased. Building on Audra Simpson's reminder that "colonialism is not a finished product,"[15] we must remember that despite ongoing colonial violence and the disruption of community-based birth practices, Indigenous families continue to grow; birthmothers and other caregivers continue to invest their love, values, and teachings into a new generation of Indigenous kin. Therefore, our intention as allies in Indigenous reproductive justice can be to hold up that love, growth, and care as a means of pushing back against the violence of settler colonial policies, to "reawaken our women to the power that is inherent in that transformative process that birth should be" (Cook 80).

That said, it is important to understand that in the process of decolonizing birth, one is not dealing with a homogenous subject ("The Indigenous Mother") but incredibly diverse Indigenous women from various sociocultural and geopolitical backgrounds. As such, Indigenous women may choose to forego customary practices even if they do have access to them for any number of reasons, and they should not be shamed for that decision. It is the ability to decide how they will give birth, where they will give birth, and who will be present during the birthing process that is crucial. Overall, Indigenous women must be free to choose. The act of Indigenous birth is, at its core, an act of radical love[16]—an affirmation of Indigenous family resilience, of Indigenous peoples' continued presence on these lands, and of Indigenous peoples' strength and futurity. Thus, in an effort to deconstruct the artificial boundaries between politics and the body, we move forward with an acknowledgement of the real decolonial possibilities that flourish when Indigenous women are given the opportunity to decide the best path forward for their unborn children.

CONCLUSION

This chapter has aimed to tell a story about Indigenous birth in Canada, and more broadly, Indigenous birth in a settler state. Indigenous storytelling sometimes has a circular quality (Cruikshank). Accordingly, we have told a story that will not conclude with a falling action but rather with a rising one. Today, we find ourselves in a historical and political moment in which community mobilization for Indigenous reproductive justice is quite literally on the rise; many communities are coming together to signal the importance of bringing customary birth practices back to their territories and regaining agency over life giving as a whole.

Though motivated by these forms of resurgence, we must continue thinking critically about the nature of that rising action, the ways in which those actions are taking place, with whom, and with what potential socioeconomic and political consequences. Both the RCAP and TRC, for example, make recommendations about Indigenous health. The TRC's "calls to action" ask that we advance the wellbeing of Indigenous communities in Canada through a process of reconciliation. The TRC's focus on reconciliation inextricably ties the project of Indigenous wellbeing to the reparation of Indigenous-settler relations. Here, we have to be cautious that the emphasis on reconciliation does not inadvertently bury assertions of Indigenous sovereignty beneath the contradictory goal of settler innocence (i.e., alleviating "white guilt") as per a nationalist agenda (Tuck and Yang; Sium et al.); this misguided formula for reconciliation forgoes the project of actually "unsettling" settler colonialism (Snelgrove et al.) which would, contrarily, require settler institutions to step aside while Indigenous peoples build and sustain their families and nations on their own terms.

That said if the Canadian government facilitated the resurgence of Indigenous birth practices instead of pushing back against them, this could represent one step toward repairing Indigenous-settler relationships. Reconciliation is often framed as a reparative process between settlers and Indigenous peoples that manifests in the strengthening of a single nation—Canada; this is a violent misconception that continues to erase Indigenous nationhood. Reconciliation should instead represent a process of building a nation-to-nation relationship between Indigenous Nations and Canada. A first step in this process requires the Canadian nation state's demonstration of respect for the very first environment, the mother's womb.

It is worthwhile to note that Indigenous midwives originally showed this respect for settler birthmothers in the early days of European settlement. For instance, Cree and Métis educator Kim Anderson offers that one of her Elder's stories tells of Indigenous midwives coming to the aid of settler women and assisting in the birth of "[not only] Indian babies, [but] Métis babies and French babies" alike (49). These excavated stories resurface a historical moment when Indigenous women offered settler life givers support in a time of need. Notably, Indigenous midwives did not seek to reform the birthing practices of these foreign women; rather, they drew upon their own traditional knowledge to ensure the safe arrival of settler children onto their land.

If we imagine an Indigenous paradigm of reciprocity presiding over the politics of birth in settler states, we might ask: how can settlers begin the work of reciprocating the kindness of Indigenous midwives that provided this invaluable contribution to their own families' origin stories in Canada? How can we hold space for Indigenous Peoples to be self-determining when it comes to birth? Tackling these kinds of questions may offer new ways of approaching our activism and engagement. By critically analyzing the relationship between reconciliation, decolonization, and birth, we can begin to explore a necessary reframing of Indigenous reproductive justice in Canada: one that combines recognition and repatriation from the settler state with an ongoing lateral flow of respectful knowledge exchanges between nations about life-giving. To achieve reproductive justice, we can learn from those early stories of Indigenous midwives and settler birthmothers who set the tone for a nation-to-nation relationship—one that did not seek to reform but to *support* each other's ways of knowing, being, and birthing.

ENDNOTES

[1]Dr. Cynthia Stirbys is Saulteaux-Cree from the Cowessess First Nation. Her master's research focused on reclaiming Aboriginal midwifery practices, and she continues examining how to optimize Indigenous women's wellness in Canada.

[2]Erika Finestone is a settler of Polish and Romanian descent and Jewish ancestry. Her family settled on the unceded territory of the Kanien'keha:ka in what is now commonly known as Montreal, and she is now a grateful visitor on the traditional territory of the WS'ANEC' (Saanich), Lkwungen (Songhees), Wyomilth (Esquimalt) peoples of the Coast Salish Nation. She is a doctoral candidate in the department of anthropology at University of Toronto, and is currently conducting research with the urban Indigenous community in Victoria, BC, on the topic of family resilience, kinship, and nationhood.

[3]For the purpose of this chapter, we have decided to use the word "woman" to describe female-bodied life givers because of the chapter's specific focus on pregnancy, birth, and motherhood. However, we are aware that this choice of language may be exclusionary to other female-identified folks who do not either have the capacity or desire to give birth. We acknowledge this choice and remain open to critical feedback about how we could frame the content of this chapter in a way that more appropriately acknowledges and honours the LGBTQIPA community. It is worthwhile to note that our focus on women and birthmothers does not connote an underestimation of the crucial role other caregivers (many of whom may not be female identified) play in the life of a child.

[4]In her book *Becoming An Ally: Breaking the Cycle of Oppression in People*, Anne Bishop gives instruction on how to critique one's own privilege and identify how it has played into other people's oppression. She describes how to use this form of reflection as a means of understanding how to be a good ally in combating those oppressive structures with the people it has disenfranchised. On her website www.becominganally.ca, she describes "being an ally" in

the following way: "Allies are people who recognize the unearned privilege they receive from society's patterns of injustice and take responsibility for changing these patterns." Our chapter borrows from this idea of allying to tease out the ways in which women of different levels of privilege can begin productive conversations and organizing around how to reform the system so that all women can more easily access reproductive justice.

[5]Dr. Willie Ermine coined the phrase the "ethical space of engagement" in his 2007 paper by that same title. He describes it in the following way: "The 'ethical space' is formed when two societies, with disparate worldviews, are poised to engage each other. It is the thought about diverse societies and the space in between them that contributes to the development of a framework for dialogue between human communities. The ethical space of engagement proposes a framework as a way of examining the diversity and positioning of Indigenous peoples and Western society in the pursuit of a relevant discussion on Indigenous legal issues and particularly to the fragile intersection of Indigenous law and Canadian legal systems" (1).

[6]RCAP recommended that all governments should base their Indigenous health policies on the following principles: holism, that is, attention to the whole person in their total environment; equity, that is, equitable access to the means of achieving health and rough equality of outcomes in health status; control by Aboriginal peoples of the lifestyle choices, institutional services and environmental conditions that support health; diversity, that is, accommodation of the cultures and histories of Aboriginal peoples that make them distinctive within Canadian society and that distinguish them from one another (5-6).

[7]There has recently been increasing reports of newborns immediately removed from "precarious" mothers at birth, often straight out of the hospital. Some of these women have open files with Children's Aid Society or the Ministry of Child and Family Development, or have been incarcerated. In one particular case at the Maple Ridge Prison where it was legally decided that inmates were allowed to "keep their babies while incarcerated," two babies born to Indigenous mothers were apprehended by the Ministry of Children and Family Development "and separated from their mothers within

hours of their birth" (Corbett). Although these women were taking part in a prison-based "prenatal education" program and "parenting programs" through a "mother-child unit" (Corbett), this training was disregarded. It was noted by Dr. Ruth Elwood Martin in personal correspondence with the prison administration that "these babies have irrevocably lost the opportunity to breastfeed and establish vital maternal-infant bonding, which research has demonstrated benefits infant development and adulthood health, and reduces recidivism for their mothers" (Corbett).

[8]Dr. Stirbys originally adapted the Bronfenbrenner socioecological model shown here for the purpose of her master's research on the reclamation of Aboriginal midwifery practices in 2006 (Stirbys, "Without").

[9]In our use of broad designations like "Western" versus "Indigenous," we mean to fulfill a specific goal of this chapter which is to begin a discussion of what makes Indigenous birth unique, especially in a settler context where dominant ideas around birth seem to disrupt Indigenous ontologies of kinship broadly and birth specifically. However, by doing so, we recognize the risk of reinforcing artificial dualities like the "West/Rest" divide that is, at times, used to further an imperialist agenda rather than disrupt it. For a more complete discussion of this topic see Chapter One of Michel-Rolph Trouillot's *Global Transformation: Anthropology and the Modern World*.

[10]This mention of the dislocation of Indigenous women from traditional territories is deliberately broad, referring to the many systematic and structural ways in which Indigenous women have been removed from their lands since European contact. Women have been dislocated in multiple violent ways: some have lost status through enfranchisement, or lost status and been forced off reserves as per Bill C-31. Some women were removed into Indian Hospitals (see Laurie Meijer Drees's book or Karen Tote's *An Act of Genocide*) land during residential schools. Today, many Indigenous girls are apprehended from their lands through the child welfare system. Many women are criminalized and institutionalized in federal prisons. There are countless ways in which Indigenous women are forcefully dislocated from land, and the subsequent limitations this places on Indigenous women's ability

to access culturally safe Indigenous birth methods should not be underestimated.

[11]Midwives work without any appropriate legislation in the Northwest Territories, Nunavut, Yukon, Prince Edward Island, New Brunswick, and Nova Scotia. Only three provinces have specific midwifery legislation: Quebec, Ontario, and Manitoba (NAHO, "Midwifery").

[12]A list of the twelve existing Indigenous birth clinics in Canada can be found on the National Aboriginal Council of Midwives (NACM) website at the following address: http://aboriginalmidwives.ca/aboriginal-midwifery/practices-in-Canada. It is worthwhile to note that in the case of British Columbia, although there are no stand-alone Aboriginal midwifery clinics, a Committee on Aboriginal Midwifery exists under the umbrella of the College of Midwives of BC.

[13]The term "obstetric violence" has been recently employed by scholars across disciplines to describe the violence experienced by women during the birth cycle, which could include one or all of the following: physical violence (for instance, a woman being drugged and restrained in order for a doctor to perform a Caesarean section without her consent); psychological violence (as in, if a woman is coerced into birth plans they are uncomfortable with); or emotional violence (for example, being shamed by medical practitioners and called "bad mothers" due to suspicions of continued substance-use during pregnancy, leaving their newborn at risk of apprehension by the ministry). For a more thorough description of some of the potential cases of obstetric violence experienced by women see Dixon's article "Obstetrics in a Time of Violence"; Berry's *Unsafe Motherhood*, or D'Greggario's "Obstetric Violence."

[14]In the book *Molded in the Image of Changing Woman: Navajo Views on the Human Body and Personhood*, Maureen Trudelle Schwarz focuses specifically on the profound spiritual importance invested in human substance (hair, saliva, fluids, blood, milk, etc.) and how these substances create and maintain a sense of Navajo personhood. It has helped our understanding of Leanne Simpson's explanation of the importance of transferring breast milk from the mother's body to the newborn's body. She explains the Maussian theory of "synecdoche" to describe this process: "the principle of

synecdoche holds that people, objects, and other entities that have contact may influence each other through the transfer of some of all of their properties. The part stands for the whole" (5).

[15]Dr. Audra Simpson powerfully spoke these words in her January 2015 colloquium presentation at the University of Toronto.

[16]The idea of "radical love" has been explored by many different authors, but most likely has its roots in queer-feminist theory and critical theology.

WORKS CITED

Anderson, Kim. *Life Stages and Native Women: Memory, Teachings, and Story Medicine.* University of Manitoba Press, 2011.

Berry, Nicole S. *Unsafe Motherhood: Mayan Maternal Mortality and Subjectivity in Post-War Guatemala.* Berghahn Books, 2013.

Bishop, Anne. *Becoming an Ally: Breaking the Cycle of Oppressing in People.* 3rd ed. Fernwood, 2015.

Bourgeault, Ivy Lynn, et al. *Reconceiving Midwifery*, edited by Ivy Lynn Bourgeault et al., McGill-Queen's University Press, 2004, pp. 3-13.

Bronfenbrenner, U. "Ecology of the Family as a Context for Human Development: Research Perspectives." *Developmental Psychology*, vol. 22, no. 6, 1986, pp. 723-43.

Bronfenbrenner, U., and A. Crouter, "The Evolution of Environmental Models in Development Research." *Handbook of Child Psychology History, Theory, and Methods*, 4th ed., edited by P.H. Mussen and W. Kessen, Wiley, 1983, pp. 357-414.

Canada and Royal Commission on Aboriginal Peoples. *Report of the Royal Commission on Aboriginal Peoples* (RCAP). Royal Commission on Aboriginal Peoples, 1996.

Canada. *The Truth and Reconciliation Commission of Canada (TRC). Honouring the Truth, Reconciling for the Future: Summary of the Final Report of the Truth and Reconciliation.* Commission of Canada. 2015.

Cook, Katsi. (Mohawk). "The Women's Dance Reclaiming Our Powers [Creation Story]." *New Voices of the Longhouse*, edited by Joseph Bruchach. Greenfield Press, 1989, pp. 79-81.

Corea, Gena. "Reproductive Control: The War Against the Womb",

The Mother Machine: Reproductive Technologies from Artificial Insemination to Artificial Wombs. 2nd. Harper and Collins. 1985.

Corbett, Neil. "Babies Taken from Moms at Maple Ridge Prison." Maple Ridge-Pitt Meadow News, 15 Sept. 2015, www.mapleridgenews.com/news/babies-taken-from-moms-at-maple-ridge-prison/. Accessed 7 Sept. 2017.

Couchie, C., and H. Nabigon. "Aboriginal Midwives Make a Difference?" *The New Midwifery: Reflections on Renaissance and Regulation*, edited F. Shroff, Women's Press, 1997, pp. 41-50.

Corntassel, Jeff. "Re-Envisioning Resurgence: Indigenous Pathways to Decolonization and Sustainable Self-Determination." *Decolonization: Indigeneity, Education & Society*, vol. 1, no. 1, 2012, pp. 86-101.

Corntassel, Jeff, et al., editors. *Everyday Acts of Resurgence: People, Places, Practices.* Daykeeper Press, 2017.

Coulthard, Glen. "Subjects of Empire: Indigenous Peoples and the 'Politics of Recognition' in Canada." *Contemporary Political Theory*, vol. 6, no. 4, 2007, pp. 437-60.

Cruikshank, Julie. *The Social Life of Stories: Narrative and Knowledge in the Yukon Territory.* University of Nebraska Press. 1998.

Daviss, Betty-Anne. "Heeding the Warnings from the Canary, the Whale, and the Inuit: A Framework for Analyzing Competing Types of Knowledge about Childbirth." *Childbirth and Authoritative Knowledge, Cross-Cultural Perspectives*, edited by R.E. Davis-Floyd and C.F. Sargent, University of California Press, 1997, pp. 442-73.

de Finney, Sandrina and Lara di Tomasso. "Editorial: Special Issue on Custom Adoptions." *First Peoples Child and Family Review*, vol. 10, no 1, 2015, pp. 19-38.

D'Gregorio, Rogelio Pérez. "Obstetric Violence: A New Legal Term Introduced in Venezuela." *International Journal of Gynecology and Obstetrics*, vol. 111, no. 3, 2010, pp. 201-02.

Dixon, Lydia Zacher. "Obstetrics in a Time of Violence: Mexican Midwives Critique Routine Hospital Practices." *Medical Anthropology Quarterly*, vol. no. 2014, pp. 437-54.

Ehrenreich, Barbaram, and Deirdre English. *Witches, Midwives, and Nurses: A History of Women Healers.* The Feminist Press. 1973.

Emberley, Julia. *Defamiliarizing the Aboriginal: Cultural Practices and Decolonization in Canada.* University of Toronto Press, 2007.

First Nations Inuit Health Branch. "Returning Safe Birthing Closer to Communities: A FNIHB Workplan for Collaboration with Provinces and Territories." Health Canada, December 2005.

Fordyce, Lauren, and Aminata Maraësa. *Risk, Reproduction, and Narratives of Experience.* Vanderbilt University Press, 2012.

Gurr, Barbara A. *Reproductive Justice: The Politics of Health Care for Native American Women.* Rutgers, 2015.

Hoover, Elizabeth, et al. "Indigenous Peoples of North America: Environmental Exposures and Reproductive Justice." *Environmental Health Perspectives*, vol.120, no.12, 2012, pp. 1645-49.

Meijer Drees, Laurie. *Healing Histories: Stories from Canada's Indian Hospitals.* The University of Alberta Press, 2013.

Midwives of Sudbury. midwivesofsudbury.ca/. Accessed 15 Aug. 2016.

National Aboriginal Health Organization (NAHO). "Celebrating Birth: Aboriginal Midwifery in Canada." National Aboriginal Health Organization. 2008.

National Aboriginal Health Organization (NAHO). "Midwifery and Aboriginal Midwifery." National Aboriginal Health Organization. 2004.

Olson, Rachel. "Restoring the Connection: Aboriginal Midwifery and Relocation for Childbirth in First Nations Communities in Canada." *The Cultural Politics of Reproduction: Migration, Health and Family Making*, edited by Maya Unnithan-Kumar and Sunil K. Khanna, Berghahn Books, 2015, pp. 169-189.

Patel, S. and I. Al-Jazairi. "Colonized Wombs." *The New Midwifery: Reflections on Renaissance and Regulation*, edited by F. Shroff, Women's Press, 1997, pp. 51-81.

Povinelli, Elizabeth. *The Cunning of Recognition: Indigenous Alterities and the Making of Australian Multiculturalism.* Duke University Press. 2002.

Ross, Rupert. *Dancing with a Ghost: Exploring Aboriginal Reality.* Penguin Canada. 2006.

Schwarz, Maureen T. *Molded in the Image of Changing Woman: Navajo Views on the Human Body and Personhood.* University of Arizona Press, 1997.

Simpson, Leanne. *Dancing On Our Turtle's Back: Stories of Nish-*

naabeg Recreation, Resurgence and a New Emergence. Arbeiter Ring Publishing. 2011.

Simpson, Audra. "On Ethnographic Refusal: Indigeneity, 'Voice' and Colonial Citizenship." *Junctures,* vol. 9, 2007, pp. 67-80.

Simpson, Audra. *Mohawk Interruptus: Political Life across the Borders of Settler States.* 2014.

Sium, Aman, et al. "Towards the Tangible Unknown: Decolonization and the Indigenous Future." *Decolonization: Indigeneity, Education, Society* vol. 1, no. 1, 2012, pp. 1-13.

Skye, Amber. "Aboriginal Midwifery: A Model for Change." *Journal of Aboriginal Health*, vol. 6, no. 1, 2010, pp. 28-37.

Snelgrove, Corey, et al. "Unsettling Settler Colonialism: The Discourse and Politics of Settlers and Solidarity with Indigenous Nations." *Decolonization: Indigeneity, Education and Society*, vol. 3, no. 2, 2014, pp. 1-32.

Society of Obstetricians and Gynaecologists of Canada. "An Aboriginal Birthing Strategy for Canada." Author. 2007.

Stirbys, Cynthia D. "Explaining the Barriers to Midwifery in Northern Ontario Aboriginal Communities through the Lens of a Socioecological Conceptual Framework." Mar. 6 2006, Unpublished paper.

Stirbys, Cynthia D. "Without Great Pain and Controversy: The Resurgence of Aboriginal Midwifery Practices in Canada." 2006, Unpublished paper.

The Truth and Reconciliation Commission of Canada. Honouring the Truth, Reconciling for the Future: Summary of the Final Report of the Truth and Reconciliation Commission of Canada. 2015.

Tote, Karen. *An Act of Genocide: Colonialism and the Sterilization of Aboriginal Women.* Fernwood Books, 2015.

Trouillot, Michel-Rolph. *Global Transformation: Anthropology and the Modern World.* Palgrave MacMillan, 2003.

Tuck, Eve, and K. Wayne Yang. "Decolonization is Not a Metaphor." *Decolonization: Indigeneity, Education and Society*, vol. 1, no. 1, 2012, pp. 1-40.

Weibe, Sarah Marie. *Everyday Exposure: Indigenous Mobilization and Environmental Justice in Canada's Chemical Valley.* University of British Columbia Press, 2016.

About the Contributors

Kim Anderson is a Métis researcher, writer, and educator with a focus on Indigenous family wellbeing in Canada. She is the author of *A Recognition of Being; Reconstructing Native Womanhood* (CSPI, 2016), *Life Stages and Native Women: Memory Teachings and Story Medicine* (University of Manitoba Press, 2011), and is the co-editor, with Robert Alexander, Innes of *Indigenous Men and Masculinities: Legacies, Identities, Regeneration* (University of Manitoba Press, 2015). Kim works as an associate professor in the Department of Family Relations and Applied Nutrition at the University of Guelph.

Jaime Cidro is an associate professor in the Department of Anthropology at the University of Winnipeg in Manitoba. She works primarily in Indigenous determinants of health in areas of food sovereignty and maternal and child health. She works in areas of birthing repatriation and more recently in community-based research on Indigenous doulas for First Nation's women who travel for birth in Manitoba. Jaime is mixed ancestry, whose father's side is Anishnawbe from northern Ontario. She has a diverse academic background with undergraduate and graduate degrees in environment and resource studies, and economic development, and a PhD in rural studies, sociology-anthropology. She was the recipient of the ACADRE/NEAHR CIHR funding for her PhD, and a NEAHR New Investigator recipient.

Leslie Dawson is completing her PhD in medical and nutritional anthropology at the Department of Anthropology at the University of Alberta (Edmonton, Alberta). Her doctoral research investigates the intersections of histories of colonization and Indigenous maternal bodies in the intergenerational developmental origins of diabetes as a health disparity among Indigenous peoples in Canada. She has worked collaboratively with the Tlicho (formerly Dogrib), a Dene people of the Northwest Territories. She has collected pregnancy and birth stories from different generations of Tlicho women to reveal the lived experiences of colonization and its impact on maternal wellbeing.

Lynda Dee Dixon is a professor in the Department of Communication at Bowling Green State University, in Ohio. Having taught public school, she completed her doctorate degree at the University of Oklahoma. Her research has focused on excluded populations, primarily women and American Indians. She is a member of the Cherokee Nation and a descendent of survivors of the Trail of Tears, a death march resulting in the losses of over four thousand men, women, and children. Her publications can be found in books, book chapters, and journal articles about prejudice, health issues, and current status of the Cherokee.

Elisabeth Dolin is a midwifery consultant, research associate and educator. Born in Wisconsin and raised in northern Manitoba, she has a midwifery practice in Canada and travels to support international efforts to advance health services for women and infants.

Erika Finestone is a settler of Polish and Romanian descent and Jewish ancestry. She is completing her doctorate in social-cultural anthropology at the University of Toronto. Her doctoral research focuses on Indigenous family resilience in Victoria, British Columbia. Erika is particularly interested in urban kinship networks and how families resist extractive child welfare interventions in ways that reflect grounded forms of Indigenous nationhood. Working collaboratively with Hulitan Family and Community Services Society, she has most recently developed a workshop called "Honouring Family Resilience" being offered at preventative service agencies and family/community organizations on Vancouver Island. Erika's journey toward this work grew through engaging more deeply with her own people's story of survival and resistance during and after the Jewish Holocaust. Her work is energized by a commitment to understand the ways in which Jewish communities are both in close kinship with—but also implicated in the continued oppression of—Indigenous communities in Canada. Through humour and open, honest dialogue, Erika strives to be an ally to Indigenous communities in Canada on whose land she is a grateful visitor.

Margaret MacDonald is an associate professor at Simon Fraser University whose research interests include intergenerational programs, pedagogical documentation, and curriculum development in early childhood education. As part of her intergenerational focus, she has been working with members of the Sto:lo and Sts'ailes First Nation in British Columbia to document language and cultural revitalization since 2007.

Rachel Olson is a citizen of the Tr'ondek Hwech'in First Nation in the Yukon. She holds a PhD in social anthropology from the University of Sussex, UK, and her research focused on Indigenous midwifery and the relocation of birth for Indigenous women in Manitoba, Canada. She is an honorary member of the National Aboriginal Council of Midwives (NACM), and has developed various Indigenous midwifery resources and research papers. Rachel is currently a member of the Indigenous Birthing Committee for the Midwives Association of British Columbia (MABC). She is also a founding director of the Firelight Group, a research consultancy working with various First Nation communities across northern Canada on issues related to health care, traditional knowledge, resource development, and Aboriginal and treaty rights.

Christina Queskekapow is a grandmother and a research assistant for university projects in her community. Born and raised in Norway House Manitoba, she has been involved in maternal and newborn Health services in her community for many years.

Terry Rentner is a professor who teaches undergraduate and graduate courses in public relations, journalism, pedagogy, and health communication in the School of Media and Communication at Bowling Green State University in Ohio. Her research in college student health has led to more than twenty state and federal grants totaling approximately $1.6 million. She has published more than fifteen refereed journal articles and book chapters, and has presented close to fifty conference papers. She will be co-editor of a book on sports communication to be published in 2018.

Sana Shahram is a Michael Smith Foundations for Health Research Postdoctoral Research Fellow with the Equity Lens in Public Health (ELPH) research project at the Centre for Addictions Research of British Columbia. Sana is also an embedded health equity scholar in Interior Health's Population and Public Health department, and a sessional instructor at the University of British Colombia (UBC) Okanagan. Her research interests include Indigenist approaches to health equity research, the social determinants of substance use during pregnancy, and knowledge mobilization that disrupts the systemic roots of inequitable health outcomes.

Naomi Simmonds is of Raukawa, Ngāti Huri descent. She is a mother of two young girls both of whom were birthed at home surrounded by family. Their placentas are buried at their ancestral home Pikitū at Te Waotu in the Central North Island of Aotearoa-New Zealand. Naomi's PhD won the New Zealand Geography Society "Best Doctoral Thesis" prize in 2014. Her thesis *Tū te Turuturu nō Hineteiwaiwa: Mana Wahine ,Geographies of Birth in Aotearoa New Zealand* considers the spatial, spiritual, and embodied experiences of birth for Māori women and their families. Naomi is also involved in tribal environmental management projects and is doing research on place-based wellness within Indigenous communities, Indigenous water values and freshwater management, and Indigenous participation in resource management. Naomi is currently a lecturer in the Geography and Environmental Planning Program at the University of Waikato.

Cynthia Stirbys is Saulteaux-Cree from the Cowessess First Nation in Saskatchewan. Having a background in Indigenous health, she has worked in areas including social determinants of health, governance, mental health and addictions, gender-based analysis, and research ethics. She has a master's of arts degree in conflict studies (Saint Paul University, Ottawa) and a PhD in feminist and gender Studies (University of Ottawa, 2016). Her PhD examined the Indian residential school phenomenon through Indigenous women's sharing of their life stories. Her research-work motivation is to optimally advance Indigenous Peoples' wellbeing. Presently, she is an adjunct professor at Simon Fraser University in the Faculty of Health Sciences, and she also facilitates workshops in support of community safety planning in northern Indigenous communities.

Rebeka Tabobondung is the editor-in-chief of *MUSKRAT Magazine*, an online Indigenous arts and culture magazine that strives to honour, investigate, and disseminate traditional knowledges in ways that inspire their reclamation. Rebeka is also a filmmaker, writer, poet, Indigenous knowledge, and oral history researcher. Rebeka's latest research and film work documents traditional birth knowledge from Wasauksing First Nation where she is also a member. Her short documentary, "Spirit of Birth" explores Indigenous birth and the Toronto Birth Centre, and is available for viewing on *MUSKRAT Magazine*.

Hannah Tait Neufeld is of mixed heritage, originally from Fort Erie, Ontario. For the past twenty years, she has worked with Indigenous women and children globally on the revitalization of traditional foods and medicines beginning in Brazil and Indonesia. At the University of Manitoba, she went on to study generational changes in prenatal food acquisition patterns, along with urban First Nations and Métis women's experiences with gestational diabetes. As a Banting Postdoctoral Research Fellow in the Indigenous Health Lab at Western University, she studied processes of environmental dispossession and their impact on the transference of traditional food knowledge in southwestern Ontario. She is currently an assistant professor of Applied Human Nutrition at the University of Guelph and focuses on health inequalities—taking into consideration community interests along with environmental factors influencing maternal health and Indigenous food systems.

Dinah A. Tetteh is an assistant professor of communication studies at Arkansas State University, having completed her PhD at Bowling Green State University in Ohio. Her research and teaching interests include health communication, women's cancers, cancer survivorship, social support, and qualitative methodology. Her work has appeared in journals such as *Women's Health, Women's Reproductive Health* and *Information Technologies and International Development*. She has presented at such conferences as the International Communication Association (ICA), National Communication Association (NCA), International Association for Relationship Research (IARR), and Kentucky Conference on Health Communication (KCHC). She is working on her first book, *"Stories of Teal: Communication and Feminist Perspectives on Ovarian Cancer,"* contracted to Lexington Books.